The Politics of Public Enterprise

The Politics
of Public Enterprise

Oil and the French State

Harvey B. Feigenbaum

Princeton University Press | Princeton, New Jersey

Published by Princeton University Press, 41 William Street,
Princeton, New Jersey 08540
In the United Kingdom: Princeton University Press, Guildford, Surrey

Library of Congress Cataloging in Publication Data will be found
on the last printed page of this book

ISBN 0-691-07677-4
ISBN 0-691-02229-1 (pbk.)

This book has been composed in Linotron Palatino type

Clothbound editions of Princeton University Press books are printed
on acid-free paper, and binding materials are chosen for strength
and durability. Paperbacks, although satisfactory for personal
collections, are not usually suitable for library rebinding

Printed in the United States of America by Princeton University
Press, Princeton, New Jersey

For my parents,
George and Vivian Feigenbaum

CONTENTS

Tables

ACKNOWLEDGMENTS

All books are, in a basic sense, the product of collective effort. This book is certainly no exception. If only one name appears on the title page it is more because of common practice than lack of gratitude to the many people whose ideas, efforts, and encouragements shaped the manuscript.

This book started as a doctoral dissertation and owes much to the teachings of the political science faculty at the University of California, Los Angeles. Moreover, the book would have been very difficult to imagine without the guidance of my friend and teacher, Ezra Suleiman. His patience and encouragement gave me the assurance to take on the luminaries of the French establishment and his own work is the inspiration for much that appears here. It is to him that I owe my greatest intellectual debt.

Stephen Krasner kept me honest. If the present argument is at all cogent, it is only because his careful reading of many drafts forced me constantly to refine and support my contentions. Given that my ideas often conflicted with his, his consistent support of the project bears witness not only to his scholarly detachment, but also to his unfailing commitment as an educator.

Hans Schollhammer at UCLA's Graduate School of Management and Richard Sisson in the Political Science Department also read the thesis with good humor and indulgence.

A number of eminent scholars read later versions of the manuscript, in whole or in part, and prevented errors of logic and fact. Peter Katzenstein was particularly generous with his time. Peter Cowhey and Nathaniel Beck enlightened me on a number of technical and not-so-technical questions. Henry Ehrmann, G. William Domhoff, Richard Sklar, and Arend Lijphart read more than politeness would dictate. John Zysman was also very encouraging.

Peter A. Gourevitch and James R. Kurth read the manuscript for Princeton University Press. They are perhaps most responsible for improving the final logic of my argument. An anonymous economist also reviewed the text for the Press and did much to sensitize me to the concerns of his profession. Sanford G. Thatcher, Assistant Director of the Press, was a great source of knowledge and encouragement throughout the process of approving the manuscript for publication, and Elizabeth Gretz, my copyeditor, made my prose a good deal more readable.

To be sure, my debts extend much further. On the other side of the Atlantic, Bruno Dethomas of *Le Monde* and Philippe Simonnot were extremely helpful in providing insights and—more mundanely—introductions to those responsible for French policy. But it is obvious that the entire project would have been impossible without the cooperation of the French officials and company executives who agreed to be interviewed. If this book takes a critical tone toward French policy, it is not meant to be a criticism of the intelligence, integrity, or commitment of those in charge. The *hauts fonctionnaires* and *grands commis de l'état* who spoke with me were in every way as impressive as the reputations that preceded them. If the story does not have heroes, it does have figures who command respect and admiration.

A Graham Foundation grant partially financed my research in France and a UCLA Foundation fellowship allowed me to write much of the initial draft without being interrupted by the usual obligations of academic life.

I would also like to thank the City University of New York and the editors of *Comparative Politics* for allowing me to reprint in Chapters 1 and 5 passages from my article,

"Public Enterprise in Comparative Perspective," and the Stanford University Press for allowing me to use Table 1.1, taken from *French Economic Growth* by J.-J. Carré, P. Dubois, and E. Malinvaud.

The considerable effort of all these people, too briefly acknowledged here, explains much of the value of the final product. The remaining defects are, of course, my own responsibility.

Finally, I would like to acknowledge the greatest contribution, that of my parents, George and Vivian Feigenbaum. Without their support not a page would have been written. Without their moral guidance not a page would have been worth reading.

INTRODUCTION

On February 11, 1982, the government of France officially nationalized five major industrial corporations and nearly all the nation's banks. This extension of the public sector formed the centerpiece of the French Socialist response to the country's economic stagnation induced by the high oil prices of the 1970s. Yet the novelty of a Socialist government after twenty-three years of conservative rule and the popularity of neoclassical economic policies among France's trading partners tended to obscure the *lack* of novelty in the Socialists' formula.

This is a book that is broadly about public policy in advanced industrial societies and narrowly about oil policy in France. Mostly, it is a book about the advantages, disadvantages, and political implications of state-owned enterprise in capitalist countries. Societies in Western Europe have increasingly turned to public enterprise as an instrument for effecting national economic policy. However, aside from the polemics of campaign literature, the political nature of these firms seems largely to have escaped the harsh light of analysis. This study examines the dynamics of public enterprise in a basic sector, the French oil industry, where there has been consistent government interest for over half a century. The aim is to illuminate the workings and the limitations of the modern state.

Chapter 1 develops a theoretical basis for our understanding of public firms and establishes the significance of the case study that follows. The first order of business here—going from the general to the specific—is to examine the range of variables that purportedly explain why states intervene in their national economies and why France has been marked by state economic intervention to a greater degree than other societies. Political culture, elite, and economic theories are examined as competing and complementary explanations. Although individually the three approaches seem dependent upon exogenous factors, taken together they can account for the high level of state intervention in the French economy.

Once a rationale for state intervention is established, the question turns to an explanation of the *form* that intervention takes; that is, why is state entrepreneurship a relevant and available instrument for French authorities? The problems that public firms are meant to address are examined in light of alternative solutions. The trend toward increased market concentration and the consequent power of the individual enterprises justify a focus of government policy at the level of the firm, as do the more traditional neoclassical concerns regarding market failure. However, economic reasoning alone does not predict the most appropriate form of state intervention. For example, problems of market failure that are solved in the United States by regulation (such as for the provision of electricity) are remedied in France by a public corporation (e.g., Electricité de France). The choice of a public corporation over other strategies (such as incentives or regulation) either to correct "natural" market failures or to bring about other socially desirable goals is essentially a political choice, because different solutions provide different distributions of benefits. To the extent that the right to appropriate a profit creates a structural conflict between the state and any private group that may wish to furnish the same service, the existence of a public firm reflects the state's capacity to impose a particular distribution of benefits. (Chapter 2 discusses this distribution for a specific regulatory solution, the French restrictions on the importation and pricing of petroleum products.) The choice of the instrument of intervention, then, reflects the constellation of forces at play in a society, particularly in relation to the power of the state.

This is what is meant by the political nature of public enterprise. Moreover, it is through the observation of public firm behavior that the popular assumption of a unified and powerful French state will be reexamined. Chapters 3 and 4 present behavior by France's integrated petroleum firms that is difficult to reconcile with the traditional concepts of public interest such as low prices, security of supply, and independence from foreign suppliers. State-owned firms, having been granted considerable managerial autonomy ostensibly for reasons of efficiency, tend to add inflationary pressures to the French economy without apparent benefits in terms of either security of supply or market independence. Managerial autonomy, an intentional decentralization of authority, added to profit maximization, leads to a structural conflict of interest between nationalized firms and the French administration. This conflict is reinforced by other elite behavior patterns. Chapter 5 notes that similar problems involving the conflict of public goals and company behavior occur in other nationalized industries in France and in other countries. Even though it is an intentional delegation of power, managerial autonomy raises the question of the state's ability to control its own enterprises. A strong, autonomous, and unified state should not have trouble controlling its own public sector. That such a breakdown in control exists suggests that both state actions and those of public firms depend upon exogenous factors. Dysfunctional policy can be explained in terms of elite conflict and inappropriate criteria for decisions (dysfunctional ideology).

These in turn force our attention to the relationship between state and society; elite networks and embracing ideology tie the state intimately to the interests of the privileged elements of society. The French state is "strong" in that it can impose sacrifices on some social groups, but it is not autonomous of *all* social groups. Although public firms may be born in moments of private sector weakness, the mechanisms that link state to society ensure that the firms will pose no threat to the organization of privilege.

This conclusion is briefly sketched in Chapter 1 and detailed in Chapter 6. The latter places the findings of this study within the broader context of the theories of the state. The clientelism and intra-administrative conflict observed seem to deny the singularity of purpose found in both neomercantilist and instrumental marxist conceptions of the state, as does the simple concept of bureaucratic conflicts between department functions—for example, Treasury versus Budget. The fact is that a belief system that justifies both a profit orientation and a large degree of independence (managerial autonomy) for nationalized firms tends to undermine the state's ability to manage economic conflict and casts doubt on the supposedly mystifying role of ideology so important to many structural marxist formulations. More importantly, structuralists emphasize the relative autonomy of state institutions to explain policies that have aided capitalism's durability. The conclusion here is that the policies of the French state bring that durability into question.

SINCE the behavior observed calls into question certain widely held beliefs about the French state, a brief note on the method of inquiry used in the study is in order. Petroleum policy in France is determined by a relatively small group of individuals whose decisions have a wide-ranging impact on French society and whose criteria of choice have important ramifications. Between October 1, 1977 and July 1, 1978, thirty-one interviews were conducted with the principal actors responsible for French petroleum policy, ranging from officials of ministerial and cabinet rank, corporation presidents, and agency heads, to middle management personnel and journalists specializing in petroleum affairs. Some were reinterviewed after the change in government in 1981. Timing limited participation by members of the Mitterrand government. All participants were promised anonymity and many spoke with surprising frankness. (Because of this promise, quotations from the interviews are not footnoted unless express permission to use the subject's name was granted.) Interviews lasted from one to two hours.

Given the small size of the sample and the type of information solicited, no survey instrument was used. The need to ask follow-up questions relating to new or previously undivulged information made a relatively unstructured interview essential. The interviews were extremely revealing about the policy process and the criteria used for making decisions and, when combined with more traditional sources of information and analysis, do much to shed light on the effectiveness of the state in an area of long and consistent government interest.[1]

---

[1] All translations from the French are my own, unless otherwise indicated.

The Politics of Public Enterprise

CHAPTER ONE

State Intervention and Public Enterprise

> La loi du laisser faire . . . soeur de la fatalité, alliée de la richesse et complice de l'injustice. . . .
>
> Georges Pompidou

Why do states intervene in their national economies? How do they intervene? Government interest in the management of complex industrial economies is now a universal phenomenon, yet reasons for economic intervention are often highly specific to the societies over which states hold stewardship. Likewise, the modes of intervention vary greatly from country to country. Public enterprise is one such mode that is widely used in France and other European countries, yet is much rarer in the United States.[1] An analysis of why this instrument is available to some states and not to others raises interesting questions about the nature of the French state, its historical evolution, and the political conditions that govern the relationship of state to society.

What follows is an argument about the political nature of public enterprise. By "public enterprise" I mean companies which either are entirely state owned or in which the state is a significant shareholder. The discussion derives first from a focus on the broad reasons for intense state intervention in France; political culture, elite theory,

[1] Public enterprise is more likely to be found at the municipal level in the United States. See William G. Shepherd, "British and United States Experience," in *Public Enterprise: Economic Analysis of Theory and Practice*, ed. William G. Shepherd (Lexington, Mass.: Lexington Books, 1976).

and economic causal explanations are examined. The political characteristics of public enterprise are then high-
lighted by contrasting state entrepreneurship with other
forms of intervention. Here it is suggested that the availability of state entrepreneurship as an option reflects the
relative power of the state vis-à-vis the private sector. When
this is further juxtaposed to the somewhat strange behavior of public firms in France, new questions are raised about
the widely assumed power and autonomy of the French
state.

Explaining the Activism of the French State

CULTURAL EXPLANATIONS

Much of the literature that attempts to explain the high
degree of state economic intervention in France emphasizes the role of tradition and political culture. Although
history does not necessarily weigh like a dead hand upon
the living, tradition is ignored at one's peril. French trans-
generational perceptions of the role and function of the
state figure prominently in many explanations because
tradition attributes value to established precedent, and
implicitly a statist tradition sways a population by its very
existence. In the French case, the statist tradition has a
venerable intellectual lineage, and has the value of historic acceptability, if not transhistoric prescription. A strong
modern role for the French state can be attributed not only
to precedent, but also to the high prestige French society
has traditionally accorded those in public service, thus fa-
cilitating government manipulation of the private sector:

> The essential French view, which goes back to well be-
> fore the Revolution of 1789, is that the effective conduct
> of a nation's economic life must depend on the concen-
> tration of power in the hands of a small number of ex-
> ceptionally able people, exercising foresight and judg-
> ment of a kind not possessed by the average successful

man of business. The long view and the wide experience, systematically analyzed by persons of authority, are the intellectual foundations of the system.[2]

Others have injected political culture analysis at the level of organization. The dynamics of groups and institutions are dissected in terms of individual behavior. State constraints and capacities then become the product of interpersonal relations. Hoffmann and Crozier, most notably, have placed great emphasis on the French aversion to "face-to-face" relations in explaining both the need for a powerful state to mediate conflict and the rigidity of the state in performing this role.[3] These traits of French society have endured over the centuries. Thus the statist tradition is maintained because it remains relevant. "Precisely because the traditional style [of authority relations] was the product of social hierarchy inherited from the feudal order, the fact that this hierarchy has not yet entirely disappeared delays the change in authority relations."[4] To explain the extensive role of the state in French society in this way gives depth to discussions of such phenomena as French versus Anglo-Saxon labor relations, or France's lack of secondary associations.[5] Tradition reinforces French public acceptance of state intervention in what might appear to foreigners as private affairs.

Of more specific relevance, the consideration of cultural

[2] Andrew Shonfield, *Modern Capitalism* (New York: Oxford University Press, 1969), pp. 71–72.

[3] Stanley Hoffmann, "Paradoxes of the French Political Culture," in *In Search of France*, Stanley Hoffmann et al. (New York: Harper & Row, 1962; Michel Crozier, *The Bureaucratic Phenomenon* (Chicago: University of Chicago Press, 1964); for a counterargument see John Zysman, *Political Strategies for Industrial Order: State, Market and Industry in France* (Berkeley and Los Angeles: University of California Press, 1977), chap. 6.

[4] Hoffmann, "Paradoxes," p. 73.

[5] William Kornhauser's keystone is assessing France's vulnerability to "mass society" in *The Politics of Mass Society* (New York: Free Press, 1959). The analysis has its roots, of course, in Tocqueville's *The Old Regime and the French Revolution*.

norms provides a greater understanding of the factors that facilitate both state intervention to promote economic development and the state's role as an entrepreneur of last resort. Contrasting America and Britain with France as it appeared at the beginning of the Fourth Republic, Landes notes:

> The concept of free enterprise, as developed in the England of the nineteenth century and transplanted to the United States, with its postulate of a competitive struggle for markets and drastic penalties for failure and with its emphasis on earning more and more for producing more and more for less and less, has never really been accepted in France. Instead, France—[of the Fourth Republic] . . . has continued to cherish the guild organization of the pre-Revolutionary period. This ideology may be summed up briefly as follows: every man has his place in society, should produce enough goods and services of quality to maintain his place, and has a right to the living earned in this manner. In other words, the justification of survival lies not in the ability to make a profit, but in the correct performance of a social function.[6]

This is in essence a Weberian explanation, attributing economic behavior to cultural imperatives.[7] Conversely, state behavior can be explained as the response to economic imperatives that have gone unheeded by a private sector whose culture makes it insensitive to the winds of economic change. This occurred, for example, with the French state's promotion of industrial concentration after World War II to meet the demands of competition in the international marketplace. From this vantage point, it ap-

---

[6] David Landes, "French Business and the Businessman: A Social and Cultural Analysis," in *Modern France: Problems of the Third and Fourth Republics*, ed. Earl Meade (New York: Russell and Russell, 1964), p. 348.

[7] Max Weber, *The Protestant Ethic and the Spirit of Capitalism* (New York: Charles Scribner's Sons, 1958).

pears that cultural norms can account at least partially for state actions.

Obviously, the existence of precedent and the enduring values of the population are extremely helpful in illuminating the reasons for France's historic state activism. However, the process of political socialization transmits a multitude of values and norms, many of them contradictory. France may have a history of state intervention in the nation's economic life that predates the Revolution, yet it also experienced a period of economic liberalism under Napoleon III[8] and oscillated between these generic solutions in the latter part of the nineteenth and early twentieth centuries. So one may legitimately ask why some practices appear relevant to policymakers and acceptable to the citizenry but other historical experiences are ignored or rejected. Theories that stress tradition and historic patterns of behavior may ignore departures from the old way of doing things. Change and innovation tend to be exogenous to the model's explanatory universe. Taken alone, the cultural approach cannot entirely explain France's high degree of state economic intervention.

ELITE THEORY EXPLANATIONS

A way of overcoming the difficulty of the cultural approach is again to disaggregate institutions to the level of individuals, this time in terms of the personnel who occupy institutional posts. Kindleberger, an implicit proponent of this approach, argues that the French economic resurgence after World War II was due "to the restaffing of the economy with new men and the new French attitudes," thereby supplementing cultural variables with an emphasis on elite circulation.[9] Here again the state is not independent but rather serves as both a summary and an

[8] E.g., The Cobden-Chevalier Treaty of 1860.
[9] Charles P. Kindleberger, "The Postwar Resurgence of the French Economy," in *In Search of France*, Stanley Hoffmann et al. (New York: Harper & Row, 1962), p. 165 and passim.

intervening variable: it summarizes by representing the aggregation of individuals in the public sector and intervenes as a recruiting and educating agent of public and private elites.[10] The virtues of this form of analysis are that it can explain policy changes where new and significant forms of elite collaboration have developed, thereby casting light on the relation of the state to its society. As Suleiman notes, "the development of oligopolistic enterprises in postwar France is . . . the result of policies that the public sector has pursued and that have been embraced by the private sector—a form of cooperation between the two sectors that represents a sharp departure from previous patterns."[11] This form of collaboration is presented as the result of coincident role perceptions promoted by recruitment from a homogeneous pool of elites and reinforced by the Grandes Ecoles, France's special professional schools, which hold a monopoly on the society's most prestigious and powerful posts.[12] In this way public and private sector elites, educated in the same schools, are imbued with the same concept of an activist state role in the economy. Both formal and informal ties facilitate this activism. Conversely, factors that divide elites can inhibit economic intervention or impede its coherence. We shall note later that this is an effect of the Grands Corps system.

Elite theory presents state behavior as the product of an intricate stimulus-response model, where the initial stimulus remains outside of the model's explanatory range. New elites may change policies because they can more

[10] See especially Ezra N. Suleiman, "Industrial Policy Formulation in France," in *Industrial Policies in Western Europe*, ed. Steven S. Warnecke and Ezra N. Suleiman (New York: Praeger, 1975); Ezra N. Suleiman, *Elites in French Society* (Princeton: Princeton University Press, 1978), part 1.

[11] Suleiman, *Elites in French Society*, p. 34.

[12] Ibid., Chap. 9. This monopoly is essentially a postwar situation. See also Ezra N. Suleiman, *Politics, Power, and Bureaucracy* (Princeton: Princeton University Press, 1974), chap. 2.

clearly read the handwriting on the wall, but the origin of the message is still unknown. To take an overly simple example, French elites after World War II may have been more sensitive to the need for a change in policy than were their predecessors. Nevertheless, it was the very different economic environment that demanded change, and the elites merely responded to these needs. The impetus to change was external to the elites themselves. Of course, policies can remain constant as long as those who want to change them lack access to positions of power, but this implies a range of structural factors that goes beyond individuals and thus beyond elite theory in its strictest form.

A network of cultural value orientations coupled to an analysis of roles and recruitment patterns goes far in explaining the French proclivity for state economic intervention. What seems to be missing, as implied above, are the economic conditions that may facilitate or even dictate a high degree of intervention.

ECONOMIC EXPLANATIONS OF STATE BEHAVIOR

It is central to the present argument that market conditions be considered in any explanation of either the level of state activity or the form state action takes. Theoretically, even classical economics accords the state specific functions. Adam Smith charged the state with the provision of certain collective goods, namely defense and the administration of justice, and of a more open category of goods that "though they may be in the highest degree advantageous to a great society, are . . . of such a nature that the profit could never repay the expense to any individual or small number of individuals."[13] In economic jargon, these are activities with significant "external ef-

[13] Adam Smith, *Wealth of Nations*, Book 5, chap. 1. See also the discussion of modern additions to this triumvirate in Carl Kaysen, "Business and Government: Do Good Fences Make Good Neighbors?" (Paper presented at a symposium on business-government relations of the American Bankers Association, Washington, D.C., 1 April 1966).

fects." In this tradition, state intervention is justified in terms of either collective goods or what is usually called "market failure."[14] Categorically, market failures are found (1) where there is a potential for important economies of scale, including natural monopolies, (2) where no consumer can be excluded (collective goods), (3) where tutelary goods (e.g., education, culture) are involved, or (4) where externalities (e.g., pollution) are important. Although these categories map preconditions for intervention by public authorities, they neither prescribe the form that such intervention should take nor equip us with an explanation for the diverse instruments available to specific societies.

However, concepts of market failure can be useful in tracing the roots of the French statist tradition. Although neoclassical economic theory has an unfortunate tendency to homogenize the diversity of societies and the distinctiveness of historical periods, specific problems that shaped the French response to and accommodation of the industrial revolution become relevant in explaining both the later readiness of officials to invoke that tradition and the array of instruments available to correct later "market failure." Arguments that focus on the role of France as a late industrializer become particularly significant. Fear of Britain's advanced industrial power added a sense of urgency to state policy. The distance between French ports and its resource centers (especially for coal, iron, and textiles) made railways a key to French industrialization, and this generally leads one to focus on the role of capital goods in the French developmental experience.[15] The role of capital

[14] E.g., Almarin Phillips, "Introduction," in *Promoting Competition in Regulated Markets,* ed. Almarin Phillips (Washington, D.C.: Brookings Institution, 1975). Regarding reasons for nationalization see Christian Stoffaës and Jacques Victorri, *Nationalisations* (Paris: Flammarion, 1977), pp. 221ff.

[15] See especially Alexander Gerschenkron, *Economic Backwardness in Historical Perspective* (New York: Praeger, 1962); Tom Kemp, *Industrialization in Nineteenth-Century Europe* (London: Longman, 1969).

goods-led industrialization in France meant vaster and more concentrated forms of investment were required and had to be developed in the absence of the more sophisticated private network of credit that Britain had developed in response to the needs of seafaring commerce. This meant that state intervention would be needed in France at least to reduce the risk of private venture capital. The state guaranteed a 4 percent return on railroad investment, providing as well both land and right of way, and thereby attracted the necessary investment; or else it carried out the investment itself.[16] (The availability of British investment capital for the establishment of railroads in the United States allowed industrialization to proceed there without a similar state role.) This form of industrialization also makes understandable the early French tolerance—if not promotion—of cartels to reduce investment risk and to permit the coordination of major basic infrastructure. A key to French state intervention is thus its relation to venture capital and investment risk. Similarly, cartelization seemed to be a way, at least over the long term, to reduce the costs of development in terms of both economies of scale and ability to attract private investment.[17]

The industrial revolution, of course, is too historically specific to provide easy explanatory formulae for an activist state. Short of an entire economic history of France since that time, this mention of the economic factors involved in the initial stages of institutional formation can at least suggest suspicions about the reasons governing present policies. In fact, the fear of advanced competition and the barriers to market entry posed by major investment requirements have hardly disappeared from the world economy; nor is the previous experience of cartel-led development insignificant today.

To recapitulate, political culture, elite theory, and an

[16] Kemp, *Industrialization*, chap. 3.

[17] See Joseph Schumpeter's defense of monopolies in *Capitalism, Socialism and Democracy* (New York: Harper Colophon Books, 1975), chap. 8.

analysis of economic conditions go far in explaining the peculiarities of French state economic intervention. Political culture analysis provides factors that facilitate state intervention because of the high prestige afforded central authorities and the value-system inhibitions to private initiative. Elite theory rectifies some of the failings of the political culture approach in that it is more dynamic and can more readily account for policy changes. Private and public elite alliances also serve to facilitate state intervention. Whereas these two approaches emphasize factors that facilitate intervention, an analysis of market conditions determines where intervention is *necessary*, given a set of goals. An array of market failures requires state intervention either to avoid the ill effects of monopoly, or to provide products or services to the community that would be unrewarding to private initiative. To understand the more positive aspects of intervention in the form of state entrepreneurial activity, the factors of capital concentration and investment risk must be taken into account. Here the state is needed to provide either large amounts of capital in the place of shallow or small-scale private sources of finance, or the assurance necessary to reduce the risk of socially desirable projects to levels acceptable to the private sector.

Why Public Enterprise?

The argument up to this point can explain the degree of state intervention in France, but not the choice of instrument. It is essential, if one is to explain the existence of public enterprise as an economic corrective, to examine the state's relation to individual firms.

CONTROL AT THE LEVEL OF THE FIRM

Although the Keynesian revolution placed the onus of avoiding economic catastrophe on the shoulders of government, simple macroeconomic intervention has come increasingly to be viewed as inadequate. The changing conditions of markets that have become notably more concentrated have cast doubt not only on neoclassical models that assume perfect competition, but also on the Keynesian prescriptions for modifying economic aggregates. Attention has been drawn to the effect of large firms both as causes for concern and as instruments of policy. A focus on what Nove calls "mezzo economics," Holland "mesoeconomics," and Galbraith the "planning system," analyses based on the peculiar dynamics of highly concentrated sectors, comes to the fore.[18] Table 1.1 illustrates French market concentration in selected sectors. The advent of concentration has produced new forms of sociopolitical as well as economic behavior. Berle and Means early noted the effects of the combined phenomena of industrial concentration and the concurrent separation of ownership and control in the U.S. structure of industry.[19] As large firms become important power centers, they are much less limited by market forces and no longer are constrained in any real sense by the legalities of ownership.[20] Major firms, often constituting an entire sector, in the absence of state intervention wield power that is responsible to nothing other than what Berle termed "the corporate conscience."[21]

[18] Alec Nove, *Efficiency Criteria for Nationalised Industries* (Toronto: University of Toronto Press, 1973); Stuart Holland, *The Socialist Challenge* (London: Quartet Books, 1975); John Kenneth Galbraith, *Economics and the Public Purpose* (New York: New American Library, 1975).

[19] A. A. Berle, Jr., and G. C. Means, *The Modern Corporation and Private Property* (New York: Macmillan, 1932). For a criticism of their conclusions, see Maurice Zeitlin, "Corporate Ownership and Control: The Large Corporation and the Capitalist Class," *American Journal of Sociology* 79 (March 1974).

[20] For a counterargument see Michael Granfield, "Concentrated Industries and Economic Performance," in *Large Corporations in a Changing Society*, ed. J. Fred Weston (New York: New York University Press, 1975). The debate can, of course, only be settled empirically. See note 28 below and Chapter 2 of this study.

[21] A. A. Berle, Jr., *Power without Property* (New York: Harcourt, Brace and World, 1959), pp. 90ff.

TABLE 1.1. Market Concentration in France

Sector	Number of Companies in 1964 (1955 = 100)	Proportion of Sales of Top 10% of Firms
mechanical industries	91	69%
automobiles, bicycles	50	90%
electrical manufactures	97	83%
chemicals	90	79%
textiles	74	74%

SOURCE: J.-J. Carré, P. Dubois, and E. Malinvaud, *French Economic Growth*, trans. John P. Hatfield (Stanford: Standford University Press, 1975), p. 169.

The relationship of property to control and therefore to power is as important as concentration in the consideration of nationalization as an instrument of policy. It is my thesis that the French state appropriates industries without controlling them. We shall see that the initial appropriation can be viewed as an index of state power, but the subsequent lack of control can only be explained by viewing state elites as ideological captives of the private sector. Before developing this point, however, the economic conditions that make public firms the logical instruments of policy need further elaboration. Given the oligopolization of certain markets, an analysis of the behavior of single firms will make the resort to public enterprise more understandable.

Microeconomics has traditionally dealt with the behavior of single enterprises, but the theory of the firm is often inadequate. Joan Robinson, for instance, has cast doubt on the theory's ability to deal with the problem of optimal size and, therefore, its ability to explain adequately either general corporate growth strategies or, more specifically, the tendency toward monopolistic behavior. Since average cost decreases with rise in output, Pigou introduced optimal size as a limiting tendency of industrial growth—that is, he introduced the notion of "diseconomies of scale" to explain why firms do not grow indefinitely. Robinson notes that although diseconomies of scale may restrain growth, the theory ignores another incentive to grow: the large firms' command of finance, "which gives them freedom to follow their own devices. . . . It destroys the basis of the doctrine that the pursuit of profit allocates resources between alternative uses to the benefit of society as a whole."[22]

Concentration justifies state attention to individual firms, and microeconomic theory gives little assurance that large firms pursuing their own interests will produce an optimal use or distribution of resources. Robinson's argument, in a sense, provides a basis for the state, ostensibly charged to ensure the general interest, to choose an instrument that will control a firm's behavior more closely than will simple macroeconomic intervention (such as interest rate manipulation). But this does not, on the face of it, suggest that state entrepreneurship—a French solution—would be more effective than a more passive response, such as regulation or selective credit allocation, to influence or control firm behavior. However, the importance of her argument remains. Uncontained corporate power, where equilibrium is not assured, does not by itself result in optimum resource allocation and thus becomes a *political* problem.

The political dimensions of the problem of highly concentrated sectors become more evident upon closer examination. Although monopoly power should not necessarily become a code word for either economic evil of antidemocratic proclivity—Schumpeter's argument for the technological benefits of monopoly is quite relevant[23]—decisions made by individual firms tend to play an increasing role in shaping the overall economy. The troublesome nature of concentration becomes compounded by the

[22]Joan Robinson, *Economic Heresies: Some Old Fashioned Questions in Economic Theory* (New York: Basic Books, 1971), p. 104.

[23]Schumpeter, *Capitalism, Socialism and Democracy,* chap. 8.

inflationary effects with which monopolistic and oligopolistic sectors are associated, and by the consequent distortion in allocating investment resources. In the case of inflation, even neoclassical theory predicts more restricted output and higher prices in monopolistic situations than in competitive situations. More importantly, monopolistic and oligopolistic control permits firms to pass on cost increases.[24] This phenomenon is not particularly tempered by the "countervailing power"[25] of unions that become partners in the benefits of sector concentration to the detriment of consumers.[26] Politically, the effects of this inflation are obvious, as groups with the least bargaining power, such as those living on fixed incomes, or working in more competitive sectors or where the level of unionization is low, suffer most.

In the case of investment allocation, as a function of concentration, individual firms account for larger and larger proportions of overall net investment. Thus the shape of the economy's future is largely determined by the investment patterns in certain highly concentrated sectors. This, of course, has been essential to any notion of state economic planning. Indeed, it has been argued that the success of planning hinges on the reduced number of participants.[27] The architecture of the society whose evolution is the charge of the state is greatly affected by investment decisions made by fewer and fewer individuals. But one is not therefore forced to conclude that the direction of investment is best manipulated by state entrepreneurship.

More specifically, solutions to certain social problems may require active participation of the state in the investment

[24] U.S. Department of Justice, Antitrust Division, *Economic Studies of Industrial Organization,* quoted in *The Closed Enterprise System,* Mark J. Green, B. C. Moore, and B. Wasserstein (New York: Grossman, 1972).

[25] Galbraith, *Economics and the Public Purpose,* p. 157.

[26] James O'Connor suggests this as fundamental to modern capitalist society in his *Fiscal Crisis of the State* (New York: St. Martin's Press, 1973).

[27] Stephen S. Cohen, *Modern Capitalist Planning: The French Model* (Berkeley and Los Angeles: University of California Press, 1977).

process. Capital may not be available to expand employment or to encourage the growth of less-developed or declining regions; the rate of growth either overall or in an industry may not be sufficient for technically feasible social projects.[28] These are often-heard justifications of state entrepreneurship, yet the state's participation need not take the form of a public firm or even a holding company. Theoretically, at least from a purely economic rationale, incentives and subventions may be equally effective in encouraging capital flows.

THE POLITICAL NATURE OF STATE ENTREPRENEURSHIP

The logic of state entrepreneurship flows from the political realm. The choice of public enterprise for policy objectives is the outgrowth not only of precedent, but of a particular constellation of power relationships. At their most basic level, nationalization and other forms of public ownership reflect a position on who can or should have the power to allocate the profits of a particular product or service.[29] A French government report, safely sheltered from any accusation of radicalism, openly noted that "nationalizations have touched at the same time enterprises where classical capitalism no longer assured profitability, and enterprises where it was desired that the profit be taken from the capitalists."[30] Incentives to unprofitable enterprises merely disguise this structural conflict; where investors receive market rates of return or similar advan-

[28] Pasquale Saracene, cited in Stuart Holland, "State Entrepreneurship and State Intervention" in *The State as Entrepreneur*, ed. Stuart Holland (New York: International Arts and Sciences Press, 1972), p. 6.

[29] The president of Electricité de France, Marcel Boiteux, stated quite plainly, "The only difference between one [public enterprise] and the other [private enterprise] is limited to the appropriation profits" (*Le Figaro*, 6 February 1977).

[30] Simon Nora, Groupe de Travail du Comité Interministériel des Entreprises Publiques, *Rapport sur les Entreprises Publiques* (Paris: Documentation Française, April 1967), p. 38. Hereafter referred to as the Nora Report.

17

TABLE 1.2. Market Failure Correctives

	Policy	Distribution of Benefits	
Increasing *state* *power*	Laissez faire	Highly skewed as a result of monopoly profits, lack of provision of social goods, etc. Least diffuse.	*Increasing diffusion of benefits*
	Incentive-disincentive schemes	Skewed; specific groups receive disproportionate benefits, although social goods are provided.	
	Regulation	Less skewed, but specific producer groups still benefit disproportionately.	
	State entre-preneurship	Benefits allocated according to political criteria, e.g., egalitarianism. Similar to criteria for use of state treasure. Most diffuse.	

NOTE: "Social goods" are any goods or services that would be desirable but are not provided in a free market.

tages in response to state incentives, the well worn left-wing complaint about the privatization of profits and the socialization of costs retains merit. Briefly sketched, several specific relations of state to industry reflect different power relationships, and different distributions of benefits. These can be categorized as: (1) laissez faire, (2) incentive-disincentive schemes (faire-faire),[31] (3) regulation, and (4) state entrepreneurship, as shown in Table 1.2. Essentially, these categories represent the power of the state relative to the private sector, where laissez faire requires little state power and state entrepreneurship much more. The categories are ideal types. Note that with the policies that require more state power, there is increasing diffusion of benefits.

Intuitively this typology offers little that is surprising, but empirically these correlations must be tempered. We need definitions for regulation and state entrepreneur-

[31] The term is John Zysman's.

ship, and these will be developed below. Such roughly hewn categories, of course, comprise assumptions about the nature of state and society that at first appear difficult to reconcile with observation. In this regard, the rubric of regulation offers some difficulty, particularly in that historical experience has led one observer to remark that, in the American case at least, "regulatory initiatives are best understood as parceling out government power to various organized economic interests to better enable them to control the public."[32] This regulatory situation has often, although not always, disguised a government-managed cartel: the U.S. Civil Aeronautics Board and the Interstate Commerce Commission are familiar examples. Thus, to present regulation as the imposition of state power on an unwilling private sector assumes that state policies reflect broad, public interests, whereas much evidence runs to the contrary. For the purposes of our typology, regulation reflective of a strong state imposes disposition of benefits not entirely desirable to the firms being regulated. The extent to which the distribution of benefits narrows suggests that state institutions become linked to the groups that benefit disproportionately.

Explaining the initiation of state entrepreneurship as the product of a particular balance of public versus private power assumes a conflict of interest between the state and private entrepreneurs. Even in relative terms this contradicts much of the literature on postwar French growth: Shonfield characterized French planning as a benevolent "conspiracy" between public and private elites, and the literature on French elites makes much of their shared perceptions and commonality of interests.[33] However, to

---

[32] Simon Lazarus, "Halfway Up from Liberalism: Regulation and Corporate Power" in *Corporate Power in America*, eds. Ralph Nader and Mark S. Green (New York: Grossman, 1973), p. 217.

[33] See, for instance, Suleiman, "Industrial Policy Formulation in France," p. 33. A most emphatic presentation of the "capture" theory is found in Grant McConnell, *Private Power and American Democracy* (New York: Vintage Books, 1966).

establish public enterprise as a kind of ideal type that represents the capacity of the state to impose a policy on the private sector, such conflict must be assumed. Nor is this totally inconsistent with observation, for although public and private elites may agree on broad issues, the details of policy bring interests into conflict. Moreover, from a historical perspective, the notion of public enterprise as an imposition on the private sector often corresponds to the early stages of the firm. As we shall see, even this initial qualification needs to be tempered. Public enterprise tends to appear in situations where the private sector is particularly weak, but the firms' operating incentives lead to a confusion of public and private interests, diverting the way in which state power is used.[34]

For the present discussion, however, we shall view public enterprise as an ideal type. We have sketched in Table 1.2 a typology of market-failure correctives that reflects increasing state power where the intention of public policy in each category is to serve broader public interests rather than narrow sectoral interests. The existence of public enterprise in this sense can tell us a good deal about the relation of state to society. That a state is able to choose public enterprise as an instrument reflects its power. *Why* it chooses public enterprise over other modes of economic intervention is another matter. As remarked earlier, many of the advantages attributed to nationalized or public firms can be attained with other instruments. Although it is true that state ownership lowers capital costs by lowering risks, the same effect can be achieved by state guarantees.[35] Di-

---

[34] Note Nove's comment that "a public monopoly if told to operate 'commercially' will tend to behave exactly the same way as a private monopoly. . . . Indeed, it can be argued that it would be worse. . . . A private monopoly is generally supervised by some sort of regulating body to prevent an abuse of its position" (Nove, *Efficiency Criteria*, p. 20).

[35] Note the discussion in John Blair, *Economic Concentration: Structure, Behavior and Public Policy* (New York: Harcourt Brace Jovanovitch, 1972), chap. 25.

recting investment to socially desirable projects or under-developed regions can be achieved by a series of incentives, usually found in the structure of taxation. Market failures, such as those that generally characterize the public utilities sector, are treated in many countries, most notably the United States, through regulation (essentially of price based on return on investment). Monopoly profits can also be taxed away.

Public firms, however, may be useful in carrying out other state goals. The Italian state conglomerate IRI has been lauded for spearheading the drive for increased standards of productivity and consequently for benefits in the competitive capacity of the Italian economy. It has also been responsible to a large extent for training of industry executives for the national economy and is one of the few Italian enterprises to make a serious effort to retrain workers who have become technologically unemployed. Indeed, in many ways, IRI has functionally substituted for state planning.[36] However, the existence of IRI is largely accidental, a heritage of the fascist past, and there is no fundamental logic that prevents its functions from being carried out by the private sector.

The economic superiority of public firms over other forms of state intervention, it seems, would have to be argued in terms of control. It may be cheaper to direct a public firm to pursue a particular activity than to provide incentives for a private firm to do the same, if only because the return on investment would find its way immediately to public coffers, and a public firm's opportunity cost would be cheaper than revenues lost through incentives. However, to argue in microeconomic terms is to miss the point of public enterprise, for the raison d'être of public firms is essentially political. Control by the public is, of course, a political relationship that is rooted in the legitimacy of the

[36] Shonfield, *Modern Capitalism*, pp. 185ff. Note also Holland, "State Entrepreneurship," pp. 1–6.

state. Implicitly, the legitimacy of state control requires a concept of public interest, without which there can be no public firm. The very existence of such firms denies neo-classical economics' only contribution to the idea of public interest, the "invisible hand." The nature of the market failure that a public firm is designed to correct may vary, leading to different structures of enterprise, but there can be no mistaking the reasoning behind its appearance. Public firms logically appear because profit-maximizing firms fail to serve the public interest. It is therefore all the more paradoxical that public enterprises in France and indeed throughout Western Europe are organized exactly as the private firms they are meant to replace. That paradox can be understood by examining the links between the state and the society from which it springs.

Public Enterprise and the Autonomy of the State: Implications for Public Firm Behavior

This study is concerned with the power of state institutions and the relationship of these institutions to the larger society. These two issues must be kept theoretically distinct. Clearly there are countries where state institutions are "strong," that is, where the state can require sacrifices by some social groups in the name of broader public goals. But these state institutions are not necessarily autonomous of *all* groups in society. France is usually placed by most students in the "strong state" category.[37] Yet though there are many varied French public institutions with specific powers of economic intervention, one need not conclude that these institutions operate in isolation from social forces.

Those who systematically address the question of state-society relations often declare themselves to be either

[37] Zysman, *Political Strategies;* Peter Katzenstein, "International Relations and Domestic Structures: The Foreign Economic Policies of Advanced Industrial States," *International Organization* 30 (Winter 1976).

22

marxists on the left,[38] or mercantilists on the right.[39] The structural school of marxists has developed the notion of the "relative autonomy" of the state in reaction to dissatisfaction with those who viewed state institutions as the simple "instrument" of the ruling class. These structuralists see the ruling class as divided, necessitating a state independent of specific capitalist groups in order to pursue the interests of the class as a whole.[40]

Similarly mercantilists, dissatisfied with the pluralist contention that state policies are merely the products of winning interest-group coalitions, have asserted that states are, or can be, independent of the morass of special interests.[41] The state in the mercantilist vision rises above the parochial needs of constituent segments of society to pursue the national interest.

It should also be noted that although mercantilists and structural marxists are similar in their assertions of state

[38] E.g., Nicos Poulantzas, *Political Power and Social Classes* (London: New Left Books, 1973); Ralph Miliband, *The State and Capitalist Society* (London: New Left Books, 1969); Fred Block, "The Ruling Class Does Not Rule: Notes on the Marxist Theory of the State," *Socialist Review*, no. 33 (1977); David A. Gold, Clarence Y. H. Lo, and Erik Olin Wright, "Recent Developments in Marxist Theories of the Capitalist State," parts 1, 2, *Monthly Review* 27 (October, November 1975).

[39] E.g., Stephen D. Krasner, *Defending the National Interest* (Princeton: Princeton University Press, 1978); Robert Gilpin, *U.S. Power and the Multinational Corporation* (New York: Basic Books, 1975).

[40] This group includes especially those influenced by the writings of Nicos Poulantzas and Louis Althusser. These in turn were influenced by the writing of Antonio Gramsci and especially by Karl Marx's *The Eighteenth Brumaire of Louis Bonaparte*. For an excellent essay on Gramsci, see Perry Anderson, "The Antinomies of Antonio Gramsci," *New Left Review*, no. 100 (November 1976-January 1977). For a criticism of Poulantzas and structuralism, see Amy Beth Bridges, "Nicos Poulantzas and the Marxist Theory of the State," *Politics and Society* 4 (Winter 1974). For an application of the structural approach, see David Abraham, *The Collapse of the Weimar Republic* (Princeton: Princeton University Press, 1981), especially Chapter 1.

[41] For the best summary of the mercantilist position, see Gilpin, *U.S. Power*, chap. 1.

autonomy, they naturally differ on what exactly they expect the state to do. Here the marxist vision is functionalist; the mercantilist approach is not.

Structural marxists see the capitalist state as fulfilling a variety of functions, from maintaining order to allow peaceful commerce, to repressing subordinate-class uprisings, to the maintenance of laws and institutions that assure the transmission of capitalist organization from one generation to the next. None of these necessarily requires an autonomous state. It is, however, necessary for the state to be independent if it is to solve problems arising from intracapitalist conflict. Since this conflict is exacerbated during periods of economic crisis, the structuralist vision chiefly diverges from the instrumentalists' in asserting the state to be an agency of conflict reduction and crisis management.[42] However, the case of French oil policy to be described seems to indicate that the state does not play this role, largely because the state's institutions have been parceled out to different sectors.

The mercantilist view of the state is not functionalist other than mandating the state to defend the national interest in international conflict. Such a mandate is so broad it defies more precise functional constraints. This model of the state, however, assumes a domestic harmony of interests that is not borne out by this study. Rather, each conflict-

[42] On the role of the state in repressing subordinate classes, see Chapter 1 of Perry Anderson, *The Lineages of the Absolutist State* (London: Verso, 1974); though not a marxist, Barrington Moore, Jr., emphasizes the peacekeeper role of the Tudor state in the development of English capitalism in Chapter 1 of *Social Origins of Dictatorship and Democracy* (Boston: Beacon Press, 1966); on structural marxists as functionalists, see Theda Skocpol, "Political Responses to Capitalist Crisis; Neo-Marxist Theories of the State and the Case of the New Deal," *Politics and Society* 10, no. 2 (1981); on the function of ideological institutions of the state, see Chapter 6 below. For a criticism of the structuralists for confusing Marx's analysis of the Eighteenth Brumaire crisis with everyday economic management, see Amy Beth Bridges, "Nicos Poulantzas and the Marxist Theory of the State."

ing group has its own vision of the national interest, each vision transferring a cost to someone else. The cost of French oil policy, we shall see, is borne by the majority of French citizens.

It is my contention that both structural marxists and mercantilists confuse state power with state autonomy. It is only by separating these concepts that one can understand the existence of French institutions and the actions of French public firms. For although the latter represents the potential for state economic manipulation in the public interest, as indicated by Table 1.2, the actual behavior of these firms has been to defend sectoral interests at the expense of the public interest. This suggests that parts of the French state have been captured in much the same way that McConnell described the supposedly weak U.S. bureaucracy.[43]

The next step is to trace the mechanism through which public policy defends private interest and the power of public enterprise becomes defused or diverted. This is the mechanism by which society controls the state. On the one hand, this control is expressed by the commitment of the state elite to the managerial autonomy of public firms and by their belief that these firms should be guided by the same commercial criteria as private firms. It will be argued, especially in Chapter 6, that this commitment to managerial autonomy and profit maximization is essentially ideological. Patterns of elite recruitment and socialization ensure diffusion of the ideology from society to state. Moreover, elite incentives to complete their careers in the private sector reinforce the link of state to society, while elites championing different sectoral interests translate the fragmentation of society into the state. Different state institutions, colonized by competing groups, are weakened by their disunity.

Furthermore, the chapters to follow present evidence that the ideology that unifies the state is ultimately dysfunc-

[43] McConnell, *Private Power.*

25

tional. Ceteris paribus, profit maximization and managerial autonomy have tended to limit the ability of the state elite to control public firms so as to implement policies in the elites' own interest. This lack of control over state enterprises vitiates the potential of these firms to correct the very market failures that are their raison d'être.

IDEOLOGY AND ELITE BEHAVIOR PATTERNS

The ideology of neoclassical economics leads the state elite to confuse concentrated markets with competitive markets. Indeed, it is the increasing concentration of markets that makes individual firms politically important and thus makes nationalization an appropriate solution. Yet, the most common distinction in the public enterprise literature is made between those firms in "competitive" sectors and those carrying out a public monopoly.[44] In a world of increasing concentration and decreasing competition this distinction may seem less relevant. Yet oligopolistic behavior is theoretically different from monopolistic behavior, and since this study deals with public firm activity in an oligopolistic market, the distinction is an important one. In oligopolies there exists at least the *potential* for competition. Exogenous constraints on policy naturally are much more important in the case where a public firm is not the only one in town. As we shall see, this competition (whether real of illusory) provides a justification for keeping a public firm on an unconfining tether. This in turn becomes the Achilles' heel of public enterprise.

Thus the highly influential 1967 Nora Report could state that "there is no reason that management of a public firm [in the competitive sector] should differ fundamentally from that of private firms. They should not . . . benefit from any special advantage or be required to submit to any obligation which distorts competition with their competitors in the purely private sector."[45] The reasoning continues as

[44] Nora Report, p. 105.
[45] Ibid.

follows. Relative loss in productivity resulting from too easy recourse to state subvention represents an inegalitarian transfer of resources from the state's tax base to consumers of the public firm's product (for example, rail service), and to the employees of that firm.[46] It is, as the Nora Report notes, a "blind transfer," less precise regarding its recipients than an instrument like taxation.[47] These considerations have lent credence to demands that public firms be constituted and managed in such a way to promote maximum efficiency and to leave social transfers to more precise instruments.

Unfortunately, it is not always easy to identify efficient operation or to find applicable criteria to judge efficiency; the microeconomic reasoning cited above often ignores precisely such phenomena as complementarity, external effects, and individuality that justify public firms in the first place.[48] More importantly, the competition posited by the Nora Report is often illusory. After all, public firms enter a sector precisely because there is a failure of the market.

The paradoxes continue. Since public firms represent a commitment of resources for political reasons, it is somewhat strange that the politicization of such firms has been bewailed. Politicization is viewed as a particular problem by those most prominent in urging the managerial autonomy of public undertakings. Of course, some forms of political interference may have little to do with the public interest considerations that first underlay the establishment of a state enterprise. The postwar nationalizations under the aegis of the Constituent Assemblies eventually were protected by statute from "political interference."[49] Experience made this understandable, for in fact technical

[46]Maurice Nussenbaum, "Comment Controller la Gestion des Entreprises Publiques," Le Monde, 29 March 1977.

[47]Nora Report, pp. 26ff.

[48]Nove, Efficiency Criteria, p. 14.

[49]David Pinkney, "The French Experiment in Nationalization, 1944–1958," in Modern France: Problems of the Third and Fourth Republics, ed. Earle Meade (New York: Russell and Russell, 1964), p. 365.

competence often figured only secondarily in the choice of public sector managers.[50]

The concept of managerial autonomy requires a corollary proviso for technically competent managers. Thus it is not surprising that the nationalized firms are headed by graduates of the "technical" Grandes Ecoles, especially the Ecole Nationale d'Administration and the Ecole Polytechnique. The degree of technical training afforded by these schools is quite questionable, but the political impact of such channels of recruitment has been singular.[51] French patterns of elite recruitment are grafted onto a structure of state-owned industry that benefits from large degrees of administrative autonomy. Ostensibly the autonomy is meant to secure greater economic efficiency, but the result is a transformation of firms into feudal empires. One beset parliamentary deputy, bemoaning this phenomenon but recognizing it as the logical outgrowth of the kind of autonomy encouraged by the Nora Report, complained that France had become "the republic of fiefdoms":

> Such [Nora Report] recommendations [now being applied] . . . form the framework of autonomy which the public authorities wish to accord progressively to each enterprise . . . but are such devices as the *contrat de programme* likely to avoid the permanent installation of these oft-denounced fiefs? Who are these men, after all, Prince of Petroleum, Duke of the Broadcasting Office, Count of French Rail . . . always of first quality, sometimes more powerful than certain ministers and who have . . . at their disposal, immense apparatuses? To whom are they responsible?[52]

[50] Pinkney notes that Communist Air minister Tillon kept the national companies populated with loyal cronies, a practice continued by succeeding parties in power, in ibid., pp. 364–365.

[51] Ezra N. Suleiman, "The Myth of Technical Expertise: Selection, Organization, and Leadership," *Comparative Politics* 10 (October 1977).

[52] Alain Grotteray in *Le Monde*, 23 October 1971. The *contrat de programme* is the formal contract defining the reciprocal rights and obligations of the state and public firm.

The question has often been asked of the corporate barons of the private sector, but the point is particularly plaintive when it refers to the sector whose raison d'être is tied to the public interest. A study of France's state-owned petroleum companies illustrates that these firms have in fact become the private reserves of particular administrative Grands Corps. These corps often operate nationalized firms for their own aggrandizement and occasionally do so at odds with the more centrally determined policy. Frequently, public firms in "competitive" sectors collude with their "competitors."[53] This elite behavior pattern has an important effect on notions of state control and state autonomy, since nationalized firms develop interests independent of the goals determined by central authorities.

Certainly, when phrased as generalities, national goals may be reconciled with a myriad of company actions. Furthermore, it is not always clear who speaks for the state; different ministries say different things. Clientelism in French ministries is well known and the indications from this study are that divisions on policy, reflecting the interests of different sectors of society, run deep within ministries. When responsibility for decisions varies, and when the interest of the President or prime minister is only intermittent, one might legitimately ask, as a parliamentary report on the oil sector did, "Where is the state?"[54]

This ambiguity in public power becomes even more of an issue as state-owned firms branch out and invest in other companies. Between 1957 and 1975 the number of companies receiving 30 percent or more of their capital from nationalized firms increased over 135 percent[55] and the next

---

[53] See Chapter 4. An examination of the phenomenon in nuclear policy is also found in Philippe Simonnot, *Les Nucléocrates* (Grenoble: Presses Universitaires de Grenoble, 1977).

[54] Julien Schvartz, rapporteur, *Rapport sur les Sociétés Pétrolières Opérant en France*, no. 1280 (Paris: Documentation Française, 1974). Hereafter referred to as the Schvartz Report.

[55] *J'Informe* (Paris), 20 October 1977.

wave of nationalizations in 1982 only multiplied this. Not only does this imply a flowering of de facto nationalizations, particularly when capital is otherwise widely held (one should recall that in modern corporations controlling interest often need not exceed 5 percent), but the accountability of subsidiaries of state-controlled holding companies becomes obscured under French laws.[56] Profits and activities can be hidden from public officials. This was an important issue when two French state petroleum firms, one with a minority of private shareholders, merged in 1975 and were so reconstituted under a state holding company that its subsidiaries became *sociétés mixtes* (partially private, and thus accountable to stockholders). It was not only the Communist Party which complained that the formerly wholly government-owned Elf had become "privatized."[57] The public sector once again moved in the direction of private interest.

INTERNATIONAL CONSTRAINTS ON POLICY

The lexicon of factors that constrain the use of public enterprise is not yet complete, for the peculiarities of the petroleum sector, the focus of the succeeding chapters, present problems that have so far been mentioned only in passing. Two salient characteristics of the petroleum industry have a bearing on the present discussion, regardless of the sociology of administrative power. State control is severely limited by the fact that the market is inherently international, at least for all non-oil producing countries, and historically oligopolistic. The former characteristic leads us to the conclusion that some of the explanatory variables for state behavior lie external to the society we are examining and to a certain extent may distort the state-society relationship we are aiming to explore. Indeed, the necessity of operating in an interna-

---

[56] *Le Monde*, 18 June 1972.

[57] The argument is most forcefully made in Philippe Simonnot, *Le Complot Pétrolier* (Paris: Editions Alain Moreau, 1976).

tional environment causes state firms to take on characteristics that are not common to other forms of public enterprise. State firms, here following the logic of the international market, begin to resemble their multinational counterparts. In more general terms:

The process of multinationalization of enterprise put the problem of relations of the state and large enterprises in a light that was unfamiliar for France. The strategy of the firm had been developed on a global scale. Its financing, its production and its personnel recruitment had also been undertaken on a global scale. Each unit of multinational enterprise, wherever it might be, had been linked in a network of interdependence with the others. This type of organization gave firms a large degree of autonomy in relation to national public authorities.[58]

Although this type of behavior is obviously not relevant to the entire public sector in France, this restructuring is the result of a shifted emphasis in public policy from using nationalized firms to pursue goals of reconstruction, sectoral leadership, or social projects, to encouraging them to compete in the international market.[59] This can be understood partially in terms of the acquisition of the same advantages of multinationalization—such as lower factor costs and escaping tariff barriers—that accrue to private enterprises. However, this sort of behavior again raises questions about the raison d'être of public firms. Renault, for example, established a financial subsidiary in Switzerland where its access to capital is less subject to the constraints of the French treasury. Reinforcement of managerial autonomy permitted by this multinationalization of

[58] Charles-Albert Michalet, "France," in *Big Business and the State: Changing Relations in Western Europe*, ed. Raymond Vernon (Cambridge: Harvard University Press, 1974), p. 125.

[59] Bernard Marois, "Le Comportement Multinationale des Entreprises Françaises Nationalisées," *Revue Française de Gestion* (March-April 1977), p. 36. See also Nora Report, pp. 25ff.

national enterprise lays the groundwork for the kind of abuse (such as collusion and falsifying information) that a National Assembly commission accused the state petroleum groups of perpetrating.[60]

The international nature of its activities may constrain a state firm from pursuing strategies that might be possible in a protected environment and thus provides an argument for the authorities to which the firm is responsible to exercise maximum flexibility. But increasing the degree of enterprise autonomy calls the general nature of the interest served by the firm even more into question. Competitive capacity can be only of instrumental value, and where a firm competes under the very special conditions of an oligopolistic market, policy may turn to pathology. Where state firms are relatively small compared to their international competition, strict observance of the rules imposed by the oligopoly may not coincide with the kinds of considerations generally thought to be in the national interest—for example, lowest possible prices, security of supply, and national independence. If public firms are mandated to maximize profits and are granted the managerial autonomy deemed necessary for this pursuit, the result under these conditions may be neither salutary nor, in the end, surprising.

WHAT seems to issue from this first look at public enterprise in France is a sense of public power gone awry. One can explain the existence of that power as the somewhat serendipitous product of the interplay of cultural, economic, and elite factors. How the power is used is partially the result of exogenous constraints such as the international environment and the limits of resources. Perhaps more importantly, the endogenous constraints— the way problems are perceived and the structure of institutions aimed at solving them—do the most to illumi-

[60]These were Schvartz Report allegations. See note 54 above.

nate why a state so apparently strong is not. Potentially powerful institutions are diverted to the service of narrow interests. We turn now to look at the details of French petroleum policy, a significant illustration of the limits of state power.

CHAPTER TWO

Regulation

> In a pluralist society this attempt to regulate
> the economy presupposes competition and
> a free market.
>
> Valéry Giscard d'Estaing

The history of the petroleum industry is a history of buc-
caneers and businessmen, of high risk and stupendous
payoffs. It has been a history that has fueled the imagination of entrepreneurs as well as the economic expansion of the western world. And although any narrative
must make reference to the occasionally cutthroat competition among participants in the oil market, the history
of petroleum is perhaps more than anything a history of
cartels.

Cartels have dominated the market for much of the
twentieth century; they have been formal and informal,
public and private. Internationally, the world of oil has been
characterized by coordinated suppliers and dependent
importers. Part of the French response to this market has
been an attempt to regulate the excesses of dependence
upon foreign oil companies. Has French regulatory policy
been successful?

It has not been successful in ensuring either security of
supply or reasonable prices. The policy seems at first to
be an example of traditional French mercantilism, but a
closer look at the history of petroleum legislation reveals
state behavior to be more consistent with manipulation by
private interests. Although proponents of mercantilism
view French regulation as the manipulation of private in-

terests for the public good,[1] an examination of the history and context of laws regulating the oil industry finds state actions to be highly beneficial to the companies while costly to the public at large.

Market Failure and Cartels: The Nature of Petroleum

The conventional wisdom of petroleum economics maintains—or at least maintained—that the cost of each additional barrel of petroleum decreases as it is drawn from an oil field.[2] It may cost a huge sum to find oil and to establish drilling operations, but pulling it out of the ground is relatively cheap: the more oil produced, the lower the cost of each new barrel.[3] This cost structure provides an incentive for each producer to extract and market as much oil as possible. In the absence of quantitative restraints for each producer, there tends to be a continual glut; as supply exceeds demand, prices plummet. The early history of petroleum illustrates this vividly: "The lives of drillers turned quickly from excitement to misery as the prices fell. The year after the first discovery the price was $20 a barrel; at the end of the year it was 10 cents a barrel, and

---

[1] E.g., Peter J. Katzenstein, "International Relations and Domestic Structures: The Foreign Economic Policies of Advanced Industrial States," *International Organization* 30 (Winter 1976).

[2] The classic work is Paul Frankel's *Essentials of Petroleum* (London: Frank Cass, 1969), originally published in 1946.

[3] The chief dissenter to this view is M. A. Adelman, *The World Petroleum Market* (Baltimore: Johns Hopkins University Press, 1972), p. 15. The implications theoretically are important. If the marginal cost of oil decreases, the market is not self-regulating and cartels are justified. If the marginal cost increases, as Adelman maintains (because cost of extraction increases) price equilibrium is possible without imposition of cartel rules. For our purposes the argument is academic, since cartels *have* come into being. Incentives exist for restrictions of supply whether or not the market tends "naturally" towards equilibrium. In the modern period of hard-to-tap oil supplies, however, the debate is important.

sometimes a barrel of oil was literally cheaper than a barrel of water."[4]

That oil men should band together in cartels would, in this light, seem understandable. Yet even if the characteristics of the market were not as disastrous as the passage seems to imply, incentives exist in any market to constrict supply and drive up prices. The high cost and geographical expanse of petroleum exploration made entry into the market difficult, and thus the companies that entered were large in size and few in number.[5] This greatly facilitated collaboration and indeed cartel agreements were frequent and widespread.[6]

Cartels need not, however, impose onerous prices. Partially, this is true because even monopolies are constrained by the limits of the demand function. At some theoretical price, people simply will not buy petroleum products, although low price elasticity means that the price can go very high before demand subsides. More importantly, a growing market stimulated by low prices can be more profitable than selling small quantities at high prices. Historically, cartel prices have been relatively high during depressions and relatively low during periods of sustained economic growth.[7]

Nor do cartels eliminate competition. Companies compete with each other for quotas.[8] Establishment of quotas

[4] Anthony Sampson, *The Seven Sisters* (London: Coronet Books, 1975), p. 39.

[5] Relative entry costs for nonintegrated firms are argued to have decreased since the 1960s. I am grateful to Peter Cowhey for emphasizing this point.

[6] Some of these, such as the Redline and Achnacarry Agreements before World War II and the Heads of Agreement after, will be discussed in Chapter 3. OPEC, formed in 1960, of course reflects the same incentives applied to producer governments, which increasingly have shared in corporate profits.

[7] Frankel, *Essentials of Petroleum*, p. 83. See also *The Index* (Quarterly Bulletin of the New York Trust Co.) 24 (Summer 1944), p. 32.

[8] Frankel, *Essentials of Petroleum*, p. 97. See also John Blair, *The Control of Oil* (New York: Vintage Books, 1976), part 1.

also provides an incentive to produce as efficiently as possible—that is, to reduce the cost of producing any given amount so that the margin between the determined price and cost of production is as large as possible.[9]

The Law of 1928

From the vantage point of economic theory, the possibility of a thriving competitive industry in oil is a question of considerable debate, both among independent economists and among those who are paid by interested parties to develop amenable theories. It is a question, however, over which the historian need not trouble himself. The evidence of anticompetitive behavior is overwhelming, and it is in this context that French petroleum policy was conceived and constructed.[10] It was with the presupposition of anticompetitive private firm behavior that the original French legislation governing the regulation of the domestic market was drawn up.

However, one needs to be more precise. The fears of anticompetitive behavior were not generated from a fear of cartels per se, because the French distribution system was already a cartel, the Cartel des Dix, a group of ten French-owned importers of petroleum products. This group had the blessing of the state and a lucrative 50 percent return on capital.[11] The fearful aspect of the *international* car-

[9]There is far from total agreement on this point. Compare Chapter 8 in Joseph Schumpeter, *Capitalism, Socialism and Democracy* (New York: Harper Colophon, 1975) with Chapter 25 in John Blair, *Economic Concentration: Structure, Behavior and Public Policy* (New York: Harcourt Brace Jovanovitch, 1972).

[10]The most famous and rigorous analysis of the historic anticompetitive behavior of the industry is the Federal Trade Commission Staff Report, *The International Petroleum Cartel* (Washington: Government Printing Office, 1952). John Blair, the principal author, brings the study up to date in part 1 of *The Control of Oil*.

[11]Edgar Faure, *Le Pétrole dans la Paix et la Guerre* (Paris: Editions de la Nouvelle Revue Critique, 1939), p. 66. The ten firms were Fenaille et

37

tel was precisely that economic power was concentrated in non-French hands. Indeed, the term "Anglo-Saxon Trust," referring mainly to Standard Oil's successors and Royal Dutch/Shell, was pervasive in the parliamentary debate surrounding the basic French regulatory Law of 1928.[12] The context in which this law was considered and passed was indeed one in which Standard Oil dominated world petroleum and was the sole supplier of the French market. Thus, organization of the French market via regulatory legislation establishing a "delegated state monopoly" (*monopole délégué*) of imports was presented as a kind of "fight fire with fire" technique: an attempt to mitigate dependence on a foreign monopoly by creating a monopsonic buyer.

Prior to the 1928 laws, with the exception of wartime measures, regulation of the market had been conceived of primarily in indirect terms, such as tariffs on refined imports. These had been rather unsuccessful attempts to promote local refining.[13]

Essentially, the regulatory legislation of 1928 had several basic tasks: to encourage refining on French territory, to promote exploration in Iraq in conjunction with the

---

Despeau, Desmarais Frères, Les Fils de A. Deutsch, La Compagnie Industrielle des Pétroles, la Raffinerie du Midi, La Société Lille-Bonnières-Coloumbes, G. Lesieur, La Compagnie Générale des Pétroles, Rafineries des Pétroles du Nord, and Bedford Petroleum. See also Daniel Murat, *L'Intervention de l'Etat dans le Secteur Pétrolier Français* (Paris: Technip, 1969), p. 9.

[12] Note, for example, the report of the Commission d'Enquête Relative à l'Organisation du Monopole des Pétroles ("Charlot Report"), *Journal Officiel*, 3 February 1928.

[13] Protection was decided by the Law of June 4, 1864. The Law of July 8, 1871, established a protective tariff of 12 francs/hectoliter. However, the effect was nominal as partially refined products could pass under the tariff barriers. Thus minimal refineries could be built to refine this "French crude." The French "refineries" of this period employed only a few hundred workers; see Faure, *Le Pétrole*, p. 63; Murat, *L'Intervention*, chap. 1.

French postwar inheritance of the Deutsche Bank's shares of the Iraq Petroleum Company (see Chapter 3), and to ensure state control of the domestic market through a state monopoly that was "delegated" to private importers via import licenses. In addition, companies regulated by this law were required to stock a three-month reserve of petroleum, to use French ships for 60 percent of their transport and, in mercantilist fashion, could be required to take on contracts for crude deemed to be in the "national interest" (implicitly less profitable) by authorities.[14]

If the 1928 law had truly been a mercantile imposition of the will of the state upon the private sector, one would have expected opposition from the oil industry. Given the interests involved, it is instructive to note the character of the opposition to the bill at the time of its passage in Parliament. There was barely a mention of the legislation in the popular press; and the specialized press, representing the viewpoint of the domestic oil industry, seemed concerned only with the customs implications of policy rather than with the imposition of a state import "monopoly."[15]

This sanguine attitude can be understood if one regards the *delegated* monopoly to be actually a political ploy aimed at preventing the state import monopoly desired by the parliamentary Left. This latter solution would have made the French government the sole importer of petroleum products giving it the bargaining power of a monopsony. Commenting on the tariff regulation bill eventually promulgated on March 16, 1928, the *Revue Pétrolifère*, voice of the industry, noted: "The import regime which should complement this legislation and which logically should have been voted first becomes little more than a relatively sec-

---

[14] This provision was extremely important after the discovery of crude in the Sahara, and will be discussed below.

[15] E. Catta and E. Lemasson, "Le Vote de la Loi de 1928," Paris: Compagnie Française des Pétroles, Service de Documentation, Note de Synthèse, Nouvelle Série, no. 2 (7 November 1977), mimeograph, p. 21.

ondary affair, if one admits that *the idea of a [state] monopoly was pretty much out of mind.*"[16] This view of the 1928 law as a victory for the domestic importing companies is further supported by noting the virulence with which the industry had opposed a state monopoly. The industry press carefully played up the faults in the Spanish import monopoly of the period.[17] The resulting "delegated monopoly" solution that established coordinated import quotas was, not surprisingly, the functional equivalent of a state-managed cartel.

Significantly, the delegated monopoly was viewed by the French companies as a way of using the state as a bargaining intermediary against the trusts. The *Revue Pétrolifère* argued in support of the device: "[Without such legislation] . . . French companies would be commercial tributaries of the Trusts, which would impose their commercial conditions and be the only beneficiaries of the technical effort accomplished by the French companies. This is, however, the situation which has created the facts."[18]

The question, of course, is why should the French oil importers (the Cartel des Dix) suddenly call for aid from the state? A glance at the market conditions is enlightening.

The 1920s were progressively characterized by an oversupply of crude petroleum, giving substance to French distributors' fears of dumping by the Majors.[19] There was

[16] Quoted in ibid. Emphasis added.

[17] *Revue Pétrolifère*, 2 July 1927 through 6 August 1927. Quoted in Catta and Lemasson, "Le Vote," Annex, pp. 14–16.

[18] *Revue Pétrolifère*, 12 October 1927, quoted in Catta and Lemasson, "Le Vote," Annex, p. 17.

[19] "Le Monde Pétrolier en 1928," *Pétrole Informations*, no. 1464 (23 February-1 March 1978), pp. 27–28. By "Majors," I refer to the largest international petroleum firms, sometimes called the "Seven Sisters." The present names of these firms are Exxon, Mobil, Royal Dutch/Shell, Texaco, Gulf, Standard Oil of California, and British Petroleum. For the best popular account, see Sampson, *The Seven Sisters*.

need for a device both to protect local companies from international competition and to prevent the French state from going "too far," for other countries were carefully considering nationalization of their local importing companies during the same year.[20]

The parliamentary debates reflected the heterogeneous nature of the opposition, some fearing too much state intervention, others not enough. In fact, the alliance of free-marketers in the Radical party with state monopolists, who were chiefly communists and diverse leftists, succeeded in delaying the legislation for over two years.[21] The left-wing opposition decried the delegated monopoly bill as a mere façade and urged the installation of a system similar to the successful wartime controls.[22] On the liberal Right, one counterproposal urged a system of licensing refineries linked to American "independents" rather than the trusts.[23]

What is important to note about the debates surrounding passage of the Law of 1928 is that the rhetorical support for the delegated monopoly was rooted in its use as a tool against the trusts. Yet its dubious potential as such a tool, later borne out by events, was recognized at the very inception of the law.

THE LAW OF 1928 IN CONTEMPORARY PERSPECTIVE

What we have seen up to this point is that the cornerstone of French interventionist (*dirigiste*) petroleum policy, the Law of 1928, was clearly desired by those subject to it. Even fifty years later French and international firms praised this system of market control via state quota-man-

[20]Principally in Latin America, but also in Poland. See Catta and Lemasson, "Le Vote."

[21]Catta and Lemasson, "Le Vote," p. 23. Notable among the fiercest opponents of the delegated monopoly were Léon Blum, Vincent Auriol, and Félix Gouin (ibid., p. 24).

[22]Ibid., p. 30.

[23]Ibid.

agement.[24] As a system of governing a cartel, it seems to fit Posner's thesis that government regulation occurs where the private cost of managing a cartel is high, at least in the cost to local French firms.[25] In the case of the French market, French importer-distributors wanted to guarantee their market positions in the face of possible attempts by international Majors to eliminate them from their own market. With a fledging national firm to protect,[26] and with a fear of international economic dependence upon buccaneering "trusts," support for this particular form of protectionism was not hard to muster. This was particularly true as the interests of the trusts were protected as well.

This latter point was duly noted by the left-wing opponents of the 1928 legislation, who urged some form of price control, at the very least.[27] However, price control is also a necessary tool of cartel management. It is the *primus inter pares* of anticompetitive practices. It was, in fact, the system of price controls that made this regulatory package acceptable to the Majors. As Adelman notes, the assurance of high product prices in France, meant to ensure the French firms "a fat profit margin—'self-financing'—is precisely what draws the detested foreigners into the French market (and others) like bees to the jam pot."[28]

[24] Note the laudatory statements by company presidents in *Pétrole Informations,* no. 1464 (23 February-1 March 1978), pp. 12–17. This is a special issue on the Law of 1928.

[25] Richard Posner, "Theories of Economic Regulation," *Bell Journal of Economics and Management Science* 5, no. 2 (1974). Posner draws heavily on the work of George Stigler.

[26] The Compagnie Françaises des Pétroles (CFP) was founded in 1924. In essence it was the crude-extracting affiliate of the French domestic distributing cartel, the Cartel des Dix, and will be discussed in Chapter 3.

[27] Catta and Lemasson, "Le Vote," pp. 29–30.

[28] M. A. Adelman, "The Multinational Corporation in World Petroleum," in *The International Corporation,* ed. Charles P. Kindleberger (Cambridge: M.I.T. Press, 1970), p. 238.

The Price of Regulation

To legitimize this deal, of course, required a *quid pro quo*, and to justify it required that the public interest appear to be served. This fell under the rubric "security of supply." Thus, the Law of 1928 was not entirely a French gift to the petroleum industry. The price exacted from the companies took several forms. As noted earlier, the 1928 law required that companies maintain at all times a three-month reserve stock of petroleum in case of emergency, submit to national interest supply contracts when deemed necessary by the state, and deliver 60 percent of incoming crude on French ships.

Although a three-month reserve may not seem to be a sufficient margin in times of supply uncertainty, it adds considerably to company cost calculations.[29] As one French company executive put it, it is a cost the companies bear in payment for the luxury of the delegated monopoly: "Take Germany, for example, where there's no obligation to maintain a reserve which costs us about 12.5 francs per ton, nor do they have a [state] monopoly. We have here a delegated monopoly where there is always the threat that the state will take back its monopoly." This became a problem for the French refinery industry in times of abundant crude. Certain independent distributors had been allowed a small market share yet, since they received their petroleum via the Rotterdam spot market, did not run up storage costs or have to absorb the relatively higher cost of sea transport via French vessels.[30] Consequently, they

[29]Israel requires a six-month reserve. This is, however, a larger reserve than most industrial countries require.

[30]The Rotterdam spot market involves odd lots of petroleum which are either left over or excluded from long-term contracts. Prices there reflect the immediate ("spot") demand for oil. As lots are small, barriers to entry into the market are low and explain the existence of these independent French companies. Only accounting for about 5 percent of the French market, firms benefiting from the "Rotterdam price" were deeply re-

43

exerted a downward pressure on prices. The threat, of course, evaporated when Rotterdam prices rose.

Although the price system was, over the long haul, highly beneficial to companies operating in France, they did suffer disadvantages in comparison with the "free market" regimes like that of Germany. First, there was a relative inflexibility of the French price fixing system and second, as executives and even some officials were quick to complain, pricing policies were subordinate to political criteria.

It will be recalled that cartels tend to have low prices in times of economic growth. The lag in raising prices to maintain profits during the post-1973 recession was actually a result of bureaucratic pricing rigidity. Typically, the president of Exxon's French affiliate complained, "In spite of the price increase accorded by public authorities on January 1 [1975], average receipts by production were still too low to cover the costs to petroleum companies and to assure a minimum return on their investment."[31]

Similarly, the relative scarcity of petroleum products resulting from the 1979 revolution in Iran sent industry representatives as far as the Elysée Palace for what they considered price relief; this time, in a novel if understandable way, they asked for the removal of price controls that had been satisfactory to them in the previous period of petroleum abundance and complacent exporting-country authorities, a move that would have raised product prices approximately 20 percent.[32] Obviously, price controls have not always operated with the industry's total approval, as will be further elaborated.

The second area of complaint about the French price

---

sented by French integrated companies, many with aging and ill-adapted refineries, confronted by massive expenses in the late 1970s economic slow-down. Their refining problems were greatly aided by the sudden supply scarcity caused by the 1979 revolution in Iran.

[31] Henri Lamaison, in *Pétrole Informations*, 18–24 April 1975, p. 27.

[32] *Le Monde*, 7 February 1979.

system is the occasional subordination of pricing decisions to political priorities. The ascendance of "political"—that is, anti-inflationary—criteria was linked to the transfer of pricing authority from the Ministry of Industry to the Ministry of Finance and the Economy. As a company executive put it, "The Ministry of Industry permitted firms a normal margin, but with the change [of pricing authority] to the Ministry of Finance we see a transfer from the entrepreneur to the consumer—where the Ministry of Finance pursues an anti-inflationary policy."

More specifically, home heating oil, gasoline, and butane figure in the consumer price index, butane being particularly important to low-income consumers. The government is particularly sensitive to areas where inflation may be attributed to specific decisions. A high-ranking official in the Office of Prices and Competition under Giscard's administration stated quite plainly: "Our product prices correspond to the indices suggested at the ministerial level. The directives which justify them are political, notably the Barre Plan."[33]

THE PROCESS OF PRICE DETERMINATION

At this point it will be helpful to consider in greater detail the process by which French domestic petroleum product prices were determined until 1982, for even though the industry complains that the situation is less favorable than under the tutelage of the Ministry of Industry, the system still has a producer bias. Prices were fixed by the Office of Prices and Competition, an arm of the Ministry of Economy and Finance under Giscard d'Estaing.[34] The process of price determination was a result of continuous consultation with industry representatives, much of the

[33] The Barre Plan was aimed at reducing inflation and was introduced just before the 1978 legislative elections.

[34] The price system was progressively liberalized under Giscard. The Socialists, however, were privately adamant about maintaining some form of price regulation.

45

contact being informal.[35] ("We are in constant contact," said a Price Office official.) In terms of participants, interest representation is highly biased in favor of the integrated companies and distributors, principally because the diversity of petroleum consumers renders them less effective and because the supervisory ministries, especially the Direction des Carburants (DICA, the Motor Fuels Office) of the Ministry of Industry, tend to support the enterprises in their charge. At this level, the Office of Prices and Competition under Giscard saw itself somewhat in the role of adversary. The following exchange with a high civil servant in that office is illustrative.

Q. Do you have differences of opinion with the Direction des Carburants? It is often said that supervisory ministries defend the interests of their industries.

A. By definition we're not on the same ground. The DICA is a defender of the profession, but it's often a question of technical problems.

Leaving aside the possibility that "technical" problems have political impacts, the Office hardly saw itself as the consumers' advocate:

Q. Who represents the interests of the consumer?

A. The consumer is not represented as such, but the National Price Council is consulted.

Q. And does this carry any weight?

A. If they presented a united front, but they have so many interests. One doesn't have the same kind of relationship with them.

When questioned further about the National Price Council (*Conseil National des Prix*), the official was unaware of

[35] During my interview with the official in the Bureau of Prices and Competition, we were interrupted twice by telephone calls from UCSIP, the principal producer-refiner interest group.

any of its members. It is in fact a committee of an extremely ad hoc nature with varying membership and irregular meetings. If the consumer is represented at all, it is by the government, particularly at election time. Of course, the industry is not the only source of complaints about the Price Office. Both the Treasury and Budget Office prefer higher prices to allow companies to finance their own investment, relieving pressure on money markets for loans or on the state for aid.[36] Of course, these reasons for opposition are minimal since petroleum firms tend to borrow on international rather than domestic money markets. What is important to note, however, is that companies find allies among their regulators, not only in the "tutelary" Ministry of Industry, but in significant portions of the awesome Ministry of Finance.

Another recompense to the government for managing the cartel is found in petroleum's contribution to the general fund; a significant fraction of state revenue is derived from petroleum products. Table 2.1 compares tariff revenue from petroleum products (tariffs are ex-refinery under French law) with general budget receipts.

What complicates the tax structure is that crude prices vacillate with the U.S. dollar, and zealous pricing officials attempt to profit from a drop in the dollar relative to the franc by raising taxes to reap the windfall. Taxes are more easily raised than reduced. Remarking on the inflexibility of the pricing system as a hindrance to reaping windfall profits, the same company executive quoted above remarked, "[State] price determination does not allow us to profit from [inflection] points in the market." Or as a Budget official sympathetic to the companies' complaint against this proclivity noted:

We also criticize [the Office of Prices and Competition for being inflexible]. It's not their fault. Rather, the sys-

---

[36] These concerns were expressed during interviews at the Treasury and Budget Offices. See Chapter 3.

TABLE 2.1. State Revenue Derived from Petroleum
Products (in millions of current francs)

Year	General Budget Receipts	Receipts from Petroleum	Percent (minus VAT)
1967	117,137	12,424	10.60
1968	125,684	12,893	10.26
1969	149,373	15,795	10.57
1970	165,260	17,304	10.47
1971	175,752	19,164	10.90
1972	198,207	20,977	10.58
1973	225,278	23,699	10.52
1974	272,984	27,366	10.02
1975	284,228	30,415	10.70
1976	342,485	33,285	9.72
1977	383,060	42,223	11.02

SOURCE: Comité Professionel du Pétrole, *Pétrole 77* (Paris: Comité Professionel du Pétrole, 1978), p. 19.

tem is absurd. We have a system biased toward short-term considerations. When the dollar is low one takes a greater proportion of taxes, but when it rises the tax is left intact. We have here a monopoly situation which leads to an absurdity: we block prices at the pump, but not the rebates the refiners pay to distributors, so the refiners lose and the consumers gain. Of course, I must say that the distributors are a very strong pressure group.

Thus, part of the regulatory problem from the point of view of the industry is that the sector being regulated does not enjoy a unity of interests, to the extent that there exist some independent distributors. As with the origins of the regulatory legislation, state actions once again tend to be protective of independent French firms against the integrated giants. Of course, these interest conflicts are really relatively minor when viewed in the broader context of the benefits of the price system to the industry as a whole.

The modifications to this system inaugurated by the Mitterrand government (see Chapter 6) further refined the system so that pricing would serve the oil industry.

IMPORT LICENSES

The conflict of interest is most apparent in the granting of import licenses. The exact impact of quotas in terms of company market shares is not immediately obvious, partially because quotas were purposefully allotted on a basis that exceeded market demand, and partially because crude coming from the "franc zone," countries which based their currencies on the French franc, was fractionally exempted from the limits of the allowance. After a careful statistical analysis, one student of French petroleum policy concluded that "these authorizations have, in practice, little immediate bearing in determining France's crude oil supply sources. They do, however, have longer-term implications which were judged sufficiently important to induce the affiliates of the international companies to appeal against the 1963 A-10 [ten-year quotas] decrees to the *Conseil d'Etat*, France's highest court in such matters."[37]

What has allowed the system to work has not been the power of the state to resolve disputes, but the continual expansion of the French domestic petroleum market. Companies that might otherwise have been dissatisfied found much to praise in a system of relative price stability—and thus minimal uncertainty—with a regular increase in absolute sales. As the president of Royal Dutch/Shell's French affiliate put it, the French regulatory system "finally assured a market where profitability was more constant than elsewhere."[38]

[37] Farid W. Saad, "France and Oil: A Contemporary Economic Study" (Ph.D. diss., M.I.T., 1969), p. 38. A-10 is the term for a ten-year import authorization. The statistical demonstration of Saad's point is found in ibid., pp. 32–38.

[38] *Le Monde*, 30 March 1978.

"NATIONAL INTEREST" CONTRACTS

"National interest" supply contracts were another way of exacting a price for the luxuries of French protective pricing. The most important use of this clause of the 1928 law concerned Algerian crude. After considerable effort and a state subsidy—approximately six billion francs—French firms, particularly ERAP, discovered significant reserves of petroleum in Algeria, then (until 1962) French territory.[39] State intervention under the auspices of the national interest contract clause was necessary for two related reasons. First, Algerian low-sulphur crude was ill-adapted to the needs of the French market and second, ERAP, the discoverer of the crude, did not have the necessary downstream distribution network.[40] The impact of these contracts was, as might be expected, to drive prices even higher.[41]

The intent of national interest supply contracts has evolved over the years that this clause of the 1928 law has been applied. Originally intended to encourage the extraction of crude payable in francs, it had the double effect of relieving the French balance of payments and cementing economic ties with nations in the franc zone; the

[39] Six billion francs is J. E. Hartshorn's estimate in his *Politics and World Oil Economics* (New York: Praeger, 1967), p. 263. It is useful to note that Elf-ERAP has gone through several name changes and organizational structures. The Régie Autonome des Pétrole (RAP) and the Bureau de Recherche de Pétrole (BRP), attached to the French Motor Fuels Office, had been formed to search for oil on French territory as early as 1939. Eventually, they were merged to form the Entreprise de Recherches et d'Activités Pétrolières (ERAP) in 1966, marketing petroleum products under the trademark "Elf" (Essences et Lubrifiants de France). After the 1977 merger with the partially private Société Nationale des Pétroles d'Aquitaine, ERAP survived as a holding company, holding the state's shares in the Société Nationale Elf-Aquitaine, the successor company. The marketing name has remained Elf throughout. See Chapter 3, esp. note 45.

[40] For an extremely detailed account of the national interest purchase system, see Saad, "France and Oil," pp. 38ff.

[41] Ibid., pp. 15ff.

emphasis in recent years has changed application of the clause both to diversify sources of supply and, after 1974, to cement political deals with specific countries.[42] The impact, however, has been the same: an increase in domestic petroleum prices.

The Impact of Regulation

It is useful to consider the impact of French regulatory protectionism on the domestic economy, at least in monetary terms. According to one economist's calculations, France paid a higher average price for total crude imports for the period of his analysis (through 1969), with the gap between France and other EEC countries widening over time. Controlled for the quality of crude petroleum sold, French prices were the highest.[43] In 1969 (that is, before the 1974 price explosion), Saad controlled for transport and quality and conservatively estimated that French crude prices were on average about two dollars more per ton than other EEC countries. This is a significant burden on the consuming public.

Increased crude prices do not necessarily imply a more lucrative market, but may simply reflect the transfer prices set by integrated companies as a function of French tax policy. That is, companies may artificially increase the price of refining in France so that the margin of profit on products sold in France is smaller, reducing the companies' tax liability. However, a comparison of multinational refining affiliates in various countries has shown French refineries to be considerably more profitable.[44]

In a perverse and nonmercantilist sense the high prices can be interpreted as an attempt to assure security of sup-

---

[42] See Chapter 3.

[43] Saad, "France and Oil," p. 171ff. Saad at first considers the year 1966 and then traces backward nine years. Although these statistics are dated, the political implications remain valid.

[44] Saad, "France and Oil," p. 193.

ply. By assuring a lucrative market to the Majors, France might benefit from the Majors' diverse sources of supply.[45] Clearly, though, the reasons for high prices have not changed since 1928. They are meant to be protective of French oil companies. As André Giraud, one-time director of the DICA and later minister for industry under Giscard d'Estaing, has said: "[French] ex-refinery prices are higher than in other countries . . . in order to maintain the self-financing of the petroleum industry. Otherwise, the French petroleum companies would no longer be able to combat the foreign companies and after a very short while this could be harmful to our economic security."[46] Recalling the 1928 parliamentary debate, an Elf executive defended the present state-administered cartel:

> In a market free from government intervention, competition is subject to the risk of *abusing competition* which is as bad in the long run as no competition. *Independent companies are threatened or disappear* in the face of companies infinitely more powerful because of excessive profit leverage, which can only be resisted by companies enjoying a particularly favorable treatment in their home countries, to an interior market with wide profit margins.[47]

The implicit justification for imposing this burden on the consuming public, both in terms of prices paid for petroleum products and in terms of the impact of petroleum prices on the rest of the economy, is the supposition that French firms are intrinsically different from the international Majors: they are assumed to be more amenable to state influence and thus more reliable in the event of an emergency. Whether this assumption has been borne out by events is the subject of the next chapter.

[45] Ibid., p. 195.
[46] Quoted in Adelman, "The Multinational Corporation in World Petroleum," p. 236.
[47] Ibid., p. 237. Emphasis in original.

PROTECTIONISM AND AUTONOMY OF THE STATE

Can a policy of protectionism be considered evidence of a strong or autonomous state? The reply is not obvious. Certainly the regulatory actions of the French state have in some instances run at counter currents to the more direct—if temporary—interests of the giant, international Majors. In a glutted market, the 1928 law's import quotas did save the local petroleum industry, but at the expense of the broader consuming public. Nevertheless, the fact that protectionism resulted in high prices without improving security of supply suggests that French regulatory policy more closely corresponds to the "capture" theory of regulation[48] than a mercantilist conception. The state may be strong in the sense that it is able to implement its policy choices, but in that the choices represent the interests of a narrow group (at the expense of everyone else), it is clear that state actions serve specific interests. Direct evidence is, of course, always problematic. There may be no "smoking gun" that reveals direct control of the administration by the private sector, but that may be because state officials *anticipate* the needs of the industry. A compatibility of world views may be the only structural link necessary. French regulatory protection appears to have meant costs for the many with benefits for the few.

[48] Cf. R. Posner, "Theories of Economic Regulation." The most elegant statement of this approach is Grant McConnell's *Private Power and American Democracy* (New York: Vintage Books, 1966).

CHAPTER THREE

Public Firms and Public Policy

> Commercial success of a public enterprise is pleasing all round, but the tendency to strive for it first and foremost may invalidate the intentions which led to its establishment in the first place.
>
> Paul Frankel

> Each public enterprise is . . . pushed to rely on itself to improve its operating environment, which leads [the enterprise] to protest its public interest obligations and to . . . emphasize . . . its own commercial interest. It all happens as if the real economic importance of nationalization is to show that among numerous private firms, certain state enterprises could prosper, so long as they were not bothered by the exigencies of the public interest.
>
> Bernard Chenot

Policy is the product of imagination and circumstance. Complex problems are rarely solved by single instruments, so it should not be surprising that the French solution to petroleum dependence is multifaceted. The instrument that concerns us here is the "national champion" firm. France has frequently adopted a policy of supporting one or two firms in a particular sector in order to give them a better chance to do battle in the international market.[1] The assumption here is that French-owned firms are

[1] See John Zysman, *Political Strategies for Industrial Order: State, Market and Industry in France* (Berkeley and Los Angeles: University of California

54

more likely to have private interests that produce public benefits (such as local employment, repatriation of profits, and local investment) or that they are more likely to accede to state demands in time of need than are foreign-based firms. It is assumed that the companies partially or totally owned by the state are an asset in the pursuit of a national petroleum policy.

What, then, are the goals of French petroleum policy and how are they served by national champion oil firms? Broadly, the goals of any oil importing country are to ensure a secure supply of petroleum at "reasonable" prices and to minimize the impact of oil imports on the national balance of payments.[2] However, the record of France's two national champions, the Compagnie Française des Pétroles (CFP) and Elf-ERAP, is mixed. Although they were created to serve the interests of public policy, they have tended to drift from their mandate as they have grown larger, more complex, and more profitable. The increasing autonomy of these firms has led them to be at cross purposes with public authorities. This, in turn, makes the characterization of France as a strong state, one that can easily devise and implement coherent strategies, rather problematic.[3] Moreover, even the government-inspired *creation* of these firms does little to justify strong-state arguments.

Press, 1977), especially Chapter 3. See also Horst Mendershausen, *Coping with the Oil Crisis* (Baltimore: Johns Hopkins University Press, 1976), pp. 52ff.

[2] Michael Tanzer, *The Political Economy of International Oil and the Underdeveloped Countries* (Boston: Beacon Press, 1969), p. 23.

[3] Cf. Peter J. Katzenstein, "International Relations and Domestic Structures: Foreign Economic Politics of Advancee Industrial States," *International Organization* 30, (Winter, 1976), and his "Introduction" and "Conclusion" in *Between Power and Plenty*, ed. Peter J. Katzenstein (Madison: University of Wisconsin Press, 1978). See also the characterization of the United States as a weak state in Stephen D. Krasner, *Defending the National Interest* (Princeton: Princeton University Press, 1978).

The Origins of the National Champions

As discussed in Chapter 1, the existence of nationalized firms in a profitable industrial sector is a reasonable index by which to judge the power of the state vis-à-vis the private sector. At first glance, the existence of two state oil companies would seem to provide evidence that French authorities can easily impose policy decisions on the private sector. However, a closer examination of the origins of the Compagnie Française des Pétroles (35 percent publicly owned) and of Elf-ERAP (100 percent publicly owned) does not bear this out. In the case of the CFP, the state was only able to impose partial nationalization when private sector forces were particularly weak. With Elf, the state enterprise was only able to penetrate in areas where private interests were essentially indifferent.

ORIGINS OF THE COMPAGNIE FRANÇAISE DES PÉTROLES

The Compagnie Française des Pétroles was originally created to manage the German share of the Turkish Petroleum Company (TPC) that had fallen as spoils to the French after World War I.[4] The structure and ownership of the firm was the result of the strategy of the Poincaré government in 1923.

A cautious man, Poincaré not unjustifiably doubted that the treasury could withstand the strain of the high risk, long-term investment needed for the management of the French portion of the TPC.[5] The obvious place to look for investors to exploit this source of crude was the Cartel des Dix, local importers who allied with the major investment banks, especially the Banque de Paris et des Pays-Bas. In the early 1920s these importers were threatened by an attempt of the international Majors to capture the French

---

[4]France received these shares as part of the San Remo Treaty of 1920.
[5]Richard F. Kuisel, *Ernest Mercier, French Technocrat* (Berkeley and Los Angeles: University of California Press, 1967), p. 30.

distribution market.[6] These private groups had originally resisted the formation of a single firm for French participation in the TPC, knowing such a device would be more vulnerable to state control. Their perceptions changed with the sudden discovery of major Iraqi oil reserves, which were the province of the TPC (later to be called IPC—Iraq Petroleum Company—with the breakup of the Ottoman Empire), and with the fear of a left-wing electoral victory in 1924. This combination of carrot and stick brought the private interests into line and the company, now named Compagnie Française des Pétroles, was chartered before the elections.[7] Poincaré's inclination against state control was reinforced by his fear that it would chase away private investors (and political allies). Thus, he ensured that formal state influence in the 1924 CFP structure would be kept to two board members (*commissaires*) named by the government.[8]

Not much later, supporters of this setup used CFP's legal status as designated holder of the Deutsche Bank's TPC shares to thwart attempts by the newly elected coalition of left-wing parties, the Cartel des Gauches to nationalize the company totally.[9] However, when the post-1929 depression set in, shareholders were confronted with a major drop in demand and possible dumping by the Majors. It was then that the state found it easy to purchase 35 percent equity in the CFP, providing it with needed cash. In doing this, the state acquired a veto on the CFP board.[10] The action was, in fact, a bailout.

What is important to notice is that the formation of the CFP in 1924 was hardly testimony to the state'a strength,

[6] Kuisel, *Ernest Mercier*, p. 24.

[7] Zysman, *Political Strategies*, p. 38.

[8] Kuisel, *Ernest Mercier*, p. 32ff.

[9] René Hubert, "Le Problème du Pétrole devant le Parlement," *Revue Politique et Parlementaire*, 143, 427 (10 June 1930), p. 384.

[10] Cf. Zysman, *Political Strategies*, p. 68. Zysman erroneously attributes 25 percent equity to the state rather than 35 percent.

but rather bore witness to the powerful influence of the private sector. The state was only able to weld the company into a potential mercantile instrument with the help of external pressure. Broadly speaking, this external pressure was in the form of the growing world economic crisis after 1929 and, more specifically, it was in the form of menacing competition from the international Majors. Thus the creation of these two supposedly powerful mercantile instruments, regulation and state entrepreneurship, was made possible because domestic and international private interests were in conflict. Apparent mercantilism was in fact an extension of protectionism. These actions, which protected domestic private interests at public expense, are what one would expect of a "weak" state.

The two forms of protectionism were, of course, closely linked. A constellation of economic conditions buttressed the logic of these two interlocking forms of state intervention. As noted in Chapter 2, the late 1920s were characterized by rising crude supplies. This both cooled the fervor of the Majors to develop crude held by the TPC and created a greater need for control of downstream distribution, putting pressure on the French distributing companies. They were confronted by the menace of price wars in which the large would swallow the small.[11] Therefore, regulation was needed to preserve the precarious position of the French distributors and to ensure an outlet for their crude-holding extension, the CFP. Just as regulation protected local firms at the downstream end (i.e., distribution), state entrepreneurship protected them by securing upstream sources of crude petroleum.

ELF

In what ways does the creation of the second state-involved petroleum group, the Entreprise de Recherches et d'Activités Pétrolières (now the Société Nationale Elf-

[11]Dumping to drive competitors from the market was a strategy of Standard Oil. In the 1920s this was still of very recent memory.

Aquitaine), reflect a similar juxtaposition of public and private power? Perhaps first, one should inquire about the need for *two* public sector oil firms. Both to secure their supply of petroleum and to lessen the influence of petroleum purchases on their balance of payments, French authorities showed more than a passing interest in locating petroleum that was either under direct French control or at least could be paid for in francs. Except for the discovery of natural gas at Lacq in the Aquitaine, geology forced exploration to overseas France, especially in the Sahara, where formations appeared most promising. However, the CFP, firmly implanted in the lucrative Middle East, was reluctant to pursue an expensive search in French North Africa. That a supposedly strong state could not prevail upon the management of a company in which it held 35 percent equity and a veto on the board to undertake a potentially profitable, though risky, activity already raises questions about state influence in its own public or semipublic sector. This will be considered later. The matter at hand, however, is to examine the conditions that created another state petroleum firm vis-à-vis the private sector.

Unlike the CFP, Elf-ERAP was from the very beginning a product of French administrative imagination. Its roots are in the National Liquid Fuel Office (ONCL) established in 1925. This agency established the Bureau de Recherche de Pétrole (BRP, the Office of Petroleum Exploration) in 1945 to coordinate various specialized petroleum operations, especially the activities of the Société Nationale des Pétroles d'Aquitaine (SNPA), created to manage the natural gas deposits at Lacq, and the Régie Autonome de Pétrole (RAP, Autonomous Petroleum Authority), created in 1939 to aid in the search for petroleum on French territory.

THE ECONOMIC ENVIRONMENT

The desire to establish a new firm is not, of course, the same thing as the capacity to do so. Establishing a new

59

state firm in a lucrative private sector is not, on the face of it, a facile accomplishment. In this context it is helpful to note the economic conditions of Elf's birth.

The change in conditions between the creation of the two firms, separated by over two decades, cannot be ignored. Yet there were similarities: both the CFP and Elf were allowed entry upon the discovery of *new* sources of crude and both had major sources of financing to develop their find. The CFP based its source of supply in Iraq with the support of the major French private financial network and Elf, as we shall see, entered the international oil market via Algeria with the direct support of the state. In both cases the 1928 regulatory act provided the firms with downstream outlets for their crude. Yet why did France need two national champions?

The answer is complicated because it really involves two subsidiary questions: first, why the appearance of another petroleum organization when a national champion already existed, and second, do the forces responsible for creating a second firm help us understand the obstacles to a merger of CFP and Elf? Part of the reason for the existence of Elf was the reluctance of CFP to search for petroleum in the then-French Sahara. This reluctance is a corollary to the success of Elf in the ordinary scramble for concessions.[12] Saharan oil was expensive. A company implanted in the Middle East, where production costs ranged from $.05 to $.30 per barrel, was likely to find the opportunity cost of investment in a region where costs were closer to five times that amount to be quite high.[13] In this sense Elf-ERAP was successful in getting what others did not want. Private firms did, of course, participate in the search for Algerian oil, but rather marginally in compari-

[12] Cf. M. A. Adelman, "The Multinational Corporation in World Petroleum," in *The International Corporation,* ed. Charles P. Kindleberger (Cambridge: M.I.T. Press, 1970), p. 229.

[13] Farid Saad, "France and Oil: A Contemporary Economic Study," Ph.D. diss., M.I.T., 1969), pp. 101ff.

son to Elf, and with the considerable enticement of an associated state subsidy program that eventually involved over $1.2 billion.[14]

Not only was the petroleum found in the Sahara relatively expensive, it was also a low-sulfur crude poorly adapted to the needs of the French market. Here the 1928 law forced French refiners to take Algerian crude as "national interest" contracts.[15]

All of these conditions indicate that private sector opposition to the establishment of a state firm would be minimal. We can thus explain the capacity of the state to impose a public enterprise in the search for and exploitation of Saharan oil. Why a second firm was necessary to do this is quite another matter. Two possible solutions suggest themselves: first, the state was too weak to either force or induce the CFP to undertake the Algerian venture, or second, there is some advantage in having two firms. These are, of course, hardly mutually exclusive explanations, and the second may be a kind of "sour grapes" rationalization for the first.

In the interviews conducted for this study, the value of having "two irons in the fire" was often given as an explanation for the existence of two firms, with the CFP considered as the French "inside man" among the Majors while Elf was to be France's "sniper" (*franc-tireur*), similar to Italy's ENI. One highly placed official close to Giscard illustrated the advantages when dealing with Britain in the North Sea: "These two groups were useful with regard to the North Sea. We had the CFP to please the Conservatives when they were in power, then we had Elf for Labour." Recognition of this kind of advantage, even in general terms, would seem rather far-sighted indeed. The same official, providing a new view of policy, noted both the power and reluctance of the CFP in 1945: "The CFP

[14] J. E. Hartshorn, *Politics and World Oil Economics* (New York: Praeger, 1967), p. 263.

[15] Saad, "France and Oil," pp. 60–64, 167–171, 200–208.

was always suspicious of ERAP. In 1945 they could have prevented the creation of a purely public enterprise if they had been more far-sighted, especially as to the exploration of Algeria. . . . Historically, the conception of the role of the state was to watch that national interests were not transgressed by a CFP decision, that is to say, a negative role."

Part of the explanation for the creation of two firms may lie within the context of elite analysis. A second firm was desired by a significant fraction of the policy elite, especially the faction led by Pierre Guillaumat. Guillaumat, the powerful *patron* of the Corps of Mining Engineers (*Corps des Mines*), was one of de Gaulle's closest advisors and is usually considered to be the chief architect of French postwar energy policy. Guillaumat was a convinced *dirigiste* and an emphatic supporter of an entirely state-owned petroleum firm. It is not, however, simply a coincidence that Guillaumat was both influential in French energy policy and a force behind France's elite Corps of Mining Engineers. It was a foregone conclusion that the high-ranking posts in the new petroleum company would go to members of this corps, which had already established a monopoly on positions in the petroleum sector.[16] The establishment and continuing life of two state oil companies therefore provided important advantages to certain elites.

To recapitulate, the foundation of Elf cannot be accounted for in simple economic terms. The very uneconomical quality of Algerian oil made the impositon of a nationalized petroleum firm possible. The same economics made Algerian oil uninteresting to the CFP which,

[16] The *Corps des Mines* is one of the prestigious Grands Corps, semi-autonomous organizations of civil servants which recruit their members from France's special professional schools, the Grandes Ecoles. The Grands Corps are extremely influential in both the French administration and the private sector. See chapter 4. For a careful study of the relationship of France's Grands Corps to the command posts of industry, see Ezra N. Suleiman, *Elites in French Society* (Princeton: Princeton University Press, 1978).

although potentially subject to the state's influence, operated totally by the same criteria as private firms. Thus the creation of Elf ultimately depended upon the policy choices of French elites: first, in their acceptance of or resignation to the CFP's recalcitrance in Algeria, in turn a function of decisions by the managerial elite; and second, in the state's decision to create Elf as an entirely public firm.

The Impact of National Champions

Did the actions of these two firms achieve the state's goal for its national petroleum policy, designed for security of supply, reasonable prices, and positive balance of payments effects? There has been a willingness in France to accept higher-priced petroleum if the source of that petroleum is more reliable, or if the price is necessarily higher to ensure the cash flow of French firms, implicitly considered to be more susceptible to the influence of Paris authorities. Likewise, state encouragement—especially financial—of exploration by the CFP and Elf, so that these companies may control their own sources of crude, has been part of the state's goal of ensuring security of supply. The goal has been to ensure that French company production globally equals French domestic consumption. Thus the president of the CFP found it important to underline in a note of praise for French policy since 1928 that "the CFP has at its disposal basic resources originating in ten or so foreign countries that is equal to more than half the petroleum consumed in France."[17] Similarly, Katzenstein found it significant that "at an estimated annual investment cost running in the hundreds of millions of dollars these policies [promoting French company exploration and production] have succeeded in creating a sizable measure of independence. In 1968 total French oil consumption exceeded total production of French com-

[17] René Granier de Lilliac, in *Pétrole Informations*, no. 1464 (23 February-1 March 1978).

panies by only a small margin."[18] Whether the companies would bring oil to France in time of need was a question answered in 1973.

THE POSITIVE ROLE OF THE CFP

Certainly the early history of the CFP bears testimony to its potential as an instrument of policy. Focusing on its origins as the French representative in the Turkish Petroleum Company, its actions in the negotiations with non-French participants in the venture easily coincided with French policy aims of ensuring crude supplies and low prices. The CFP ensured these not only by agreeing to buy the portion of crude corresponding to Calouste Gulbenkian's 5 percent share in the TPC, thereby expanding France's access to crude, but also by the price and the rate at which oil was extracted for the French home market.[19] This was clear from an American government report that had access to confidential sources:

> Basically, the difference between the parties was that Shell, Anglo-Persian and NEDC [the American Majors] wanted a high price for IPC [i.e., TPC] crude, which meant that they could amortize expenses and earn a return on capital with a relatively small output, while the French were interested in a low price for oil and a long period for depreciation and amortizing expenses, which would have the effect of inducing a larger production from the IPC in order to cover expenses and a return on

[18] Peter J. Katzenstein, "International Relations and Domestic Structures," p. 37. Adelman estimates the investment at closer to $1 billion per year in *World Petroleum Market*, p. 237.

[19] Gulbenkian, the independent Armenian oil magnate ("Mr. Five Percent"), had no refining facilities. His complementary interests were to make him a continual ally of the CFP in disputes with the Majors. For the most careful analysis of the TPC negotiations, see United States Federal Trade Commission Staff Report, *The International Petroleum Cartel* (Washington: Government Printing Office, 1952), pp. 54ff. Hereafter cited as FTC Report. John Blair was principal author.

investment. The three major groups were also afraid that if Iraq crude were delivered at a low price the French might use the low price of Iraq oil as a means of influencing the product prices in France.[20]

Presumably, were the CFP only defending its interest as a private, profit-maximizing corporation, there would be little reason for it to defect from the oligopoly tactics of its partners. However, both low prices and greater lifting of crude fit reasonably within the policy goals outlined above.

Along the same lines, but perhaps even more significantly, the CFP refused to adhere to the principles of the Achnacarry Agreement of 1928 in which the Majors formalized the international cartel, specifically with regard to setting prices, quotas, and enforcement procedures.[21] However, the refusal to apply the principles of the Achnacarry Agreement may be more significant in the clue it provides to the coincident interests of the French company and the French state. Certainly, the refusal to accede to the agreement was not based on any aversion to cartels in principle. Only a few years earlier, CFP representatives had negotiated fiercely with their IPC partners to control entry rigorously to the entire Middle East, in counterpoint to the American demand for an "open door" to the defunct Ottoman Empire.[22] Aided by the post-1925 oil glut, the CFP succeeded in building into the IPC a "self-denying" clause restricting entry into and guaranteeing the CFP a share of an area designated on the map by a red line. The red line enclosed the entire Ottoman Empire.[23]

Essentially, CFP actions can be understood in terms of classic cartel behavior. The Red Line Agreement not only sheltered the CFP from competition, but guaranteed considerable room for expansion in absolute terms. It pro-

[20] FTC Report, p. 76.
[21] Ibid., p. 74.
[22] Ibid., p. 78.
[23] The Red Line Agreement was concluded July 31, 1928.

65

tected the fledgling company from the potentially intense scramble for concessions where the Majors were formidably armed, both financially and technically, to squeeze the French from the subsoil wealth of Arabia.

The circumstances of the Achnacarry Agreement offered the CFP no similar advantage. The agreement was designed to guarantee the profitability of downstream operations. The evolution of the CFP can be understood by noting Frankel's observations concerning the polarity of a cartel's "insiders" and "outsiders":

> Nobody can be in a better position than he [the "outsider"] whose price is protected by self-denial of others, but whose trade and volume is unrestricted . . . but alas! the more successful he becomes, the greater his danger of cutting off the branch upon which he is sitting.
>
> . . . Thus, while the position of the biggest "outsider" is the most desirable, the lot of the smallest "insider" is the most uncomfortable. . . . In the technical and in the distribution sphere he finds it difficult to keep up with his bigger brothers, yet he is deprived of that natural weapon of the interloper, the underselling of his competition.[24]

The Achnacarry Agreement, therefore, represented a cartel where the CFP could be a growing "outsider." As it grew to be an eighth Sister, however, its effect on markets became more and more discernable and thus it developed an interest in cooperating with the Majors. In fact, by 1936 more than 42 percent of France's crude oil came from the IPC, 20 percent of which was refined by the Compagnie Française de Raffinage (CFR), the CFP's downstream affiliate.[25]

By the end of World War II, identification of the CFP with the interests of a cartel was so complete that when

[24] Paul H. Frankel, *Essentials of Petroleum* (London: Frank Cass, 1969), p. 86.

[25] Kuisel, *Ernest Mercier*, p. 44.

the Americans attempted to abrogate the Red Line Agreement, ostensibly because the CFP had become an "enemy agent" for the Vichy regime, the CFP fought tooth and nail to stay in the cartel and effectively renegotiated market restrictions within a format called the "Heads of Agreement" in 1948.[26] The postwar collaboration with the Majors in their search for new sources of crude perhaps paid off most substantially after the CIA-engineered coup in Iran in 1953, which resulted in a "spectacular increase in exports" to the benefit of the new Iranian Consortium, of which the CFP held 6 percent.[27] This is not to say the company was satisfied: de Montaigne, a former CFP managing director, notes that consortium rules did not always "permit the CFP to commercialize the amount of Iranian tonnage it felt necessary."[28] However, Blair shows not only the rigor with which the CFP adhered to those rules, but the integral part it played in determining the capacity of the consortium: in the fifteen years from 1957 to 1971 (inclusive), the CFP's yearly lifting bid (that is, its estimate of crude it would need from the consortium based on its own demand projections) became the standard for the consortium nine times, or 60 percent of the period.[29] This should not be construed as indicating that the CFP had greater control of the consortium than its partners, but rather that the decisions of the cartel were often optimal from the point of view of the French company.

However, it is not enough simply to list the benefits accruing to the CFP from its association with the Majors. One needs to continue to consider this behavior in light of the French interests. The considerable postwar expansion of

[26] Jean Rondot, La Compagnie Française des Pétroles, (Paris: Plon, 1962), p. 67; see also FTC Report, p. 112.

[27] René de Montaigne, "Présence Pétrolière de la France au Proche Orient," Revue Française de l'Energie, no. 215 (October-November 1969), p. 137.

[28] Ibid.

[29] John Blair, The Control of Oil (New York: Vintage Books, 1976), pp. 106–107.

the CFP was not simply a function of profit maximization, but reflected again a coincidence of public and private interests. Postwar scarcity and the conscious European shift from coal to petroleum[30] not only meant a need for new sources of crude, but also a need for new sources of foreign exchange in light of the heavy import bill from the United States and the resulting "dollar gap." While the Compagnie Française des Pétroles was lethargic in its search for oil that could be purchased with French francs (although it did create an Algerian affiliate to do some exploration in the Sahara), and drew the major source of its crude from the sterling area (Iraq), the CFP did make an effort to establish downstream facilities in areas where it could earn hard currency, especially sterling. Thus the CFP established downstream operations, especially of distribution, in Nigeria, South Africa, New Zealand, and Australia to earn hard currency, while maintaining the Middle East as its chief source of crude.[31]

THE POSITIVE ROLE OF ELF-ERAP

Similarly, the Entreprise de Recherches et d'Activités Pétrolières (ERAP) was very much the instrument of public policy. Created for a specific purpose, there was no way the company could, at least originally, escape its mandate. The company's main task was to assure security of supply with oil that could be paid for in francs. Although the original state firms (BRP, RAP, and SNPA) could search for oil in Algeria as separate units, they were merged, presumably for reasons of managerial synergism, by the Decree of December 17, 1965.[32] These companies thus

[30] See, for example, Dankwart Rustow, "Europe in the Age of Petroleum," in *Industrial Policies in Western Europe*, eds. Steven J. Warnecke and Ezra N. Suleiman (New York: Praeger, 1975).

[31] Rondot, *La Compagnie Française*, chap. 10.

[32] The merger was justified in terms of *size* by Elf's first annual report: "In an industry where everything takes place on a world scale and where for the first fifty years a rigorous selection has only left the largest enterprises; at a time when the Common Market enters its final phase, when

constituted, as an integrated group, the amalgam of various state-interested operations in exploration, extraction, refining, and distribution. Elf seems, by the state's own criteria, to have complied with administrative expectations. It found, extracted, refined, and distributed crude from the franc area and expanded as much as possible in as many crude-producing areas as possible. The company was able to do this through both the influence of French foreign policy (state-to-state contracts) and through a particularly innovative approach to contracting and concessions. For the latter, ERAP was able to gain access to new sources of crude by concluding *contrats d'entreprise* with Iran in 1966 and Iraq in 1968, which were essentially management contracts rather than concessionary agreements, the major difference being the greater control and more favorable terms accorded the host country.[33] Similar contracts, *contrats d'association*, were concluded with Algeria in 1965 and Libya in 1968. Elf also established affiliates in Australia, Canada, the North Sea, but perhaps most importantly on the Gulf of Guinea in Nigeria and Gabon. Elf-Gabon, in fact, is listed separately on the Paris stock exchange and the bargain prices it pays to Gabon allow Elf the largest cash flow of any French corporation.[34]

---

competition on the European market reaches worrisome proportions, such a merger of French public petroleum firms responds to an obvious necessity" (Entreprise de Recherche et d'Activités Pétrolières, *Rapport de Gestion*, Paris, 1966, p. 6).

[33] For the text of the contract with the Iraqi National Oil Company in English see Organization of Petroleum Exporting Countries, *Selected Documents of the International Petroleum Industry 1968* (Vienna: OPEC, 1969), pp. 107ff. For a discussion of the contracts, see Julien Schvartz, rapporteur, *Rapport sur les Sociétés Pétrolières Opérant en France*, Assemblée Nationale, Annexe au procès-verbal de la séance du 6 novembre 1974, no. 1280 (Paris: Documentation Française, 1974) Tome 2, p. 196. (Hereafter cited as the Schvartz Report.)

[34] Although Elf was totally state owned until 1976, many of its affiliates were joint ventures or privately subscribed. The most significant of these

Even with such commercially interesting contracts it is doubtful whether the company could have secured these additions without the support of French foreign policy. For example, the Libyan agreement was achieved through a considerable grant to the Libyan national oil company, and the leaders of Gabon were (and are) totally dependent upon the French for their security.[35]

Since Elf itself was beneficiary of a generous subsidy,[36] it would be hard to class ERAP's actions under the rubric of simple commercial relations. The role of the French state was even clearer in the accords concluded with Algeria, which was the first example of a state-to-state petroleum contract. Elf was, in fact, merely the vehicle chosen to implement the 1965 cooperation agreement between France and Algeria, which essentially granted a substantial concession of Algerian crude under terms of host country taxation that were highly favorable to the French firm.[37] Even when French petroleum production assets in Algeria were nationalized in 1971 and inadequate compensation translated into almost a two-thirds confiscation by some calculations, ERAP continued its operations there, albeit under considerably less lucrative conditions.[38]

Thus it would appear that ERAP, a creature of state policy, duly served its creator. Under its earlier incarnations

---

was the Société Nationale des Pétroles d'Aquitaine, 49 percent of which was held privately.

[35] Schvartz Report, Tome 2, p. 196. Of course, the United States similarly subsidized OPEC countries via its foreign tax credit. See Stephen D. Krasner, "A Statist Interpretation of American Oil Policy toward the Middle East," *Political Science Quarterly* 94 (Spring 1979), p. 87.

[36] Especially through the *Fonds de Soutien des Hydrocarbures*.

[37] France promised substantial aid to Algeria's industrial development in exchange for these lucrative terms (Schvartz Report, Tome 2, p. 202). Whether the promise was kept is a matter of some debate; Pierre Judet, "La Détérioration des Relations entre la France et l'Algérie," *Le Monde Diplomatique* (February 1976).

[38] Katzenstein, "International Relations," p. 38.

it sought, found, and commercialized Algerian petroleum. Under a mandate to diversify its sources of supply, it did just that. Yet the record of more recent events seems to call into question the relationship of public firms to public policy.

Public Companies and Public Goals: Negative Aspects

THE SCHVARTZ REPORT

Most obvious of indications that there exists a divergence between policy goals and public firm actions was the publication in 1974 of the National Assembly's Schvartz Report on petroleum firms operating in France.[39] Although it was no accident that the report was signed by a deputy from a coal-producing region and largely saw light because it favored the position of anti-Giscard Gaullists and the left-wing opposition, the report nevertheless raised interesting questions about the relationship of the CFP and Elf to the state. The report alleged conduct on the part of these companies that hardly seemed in keeping with a public interest mandate. It accused the companies of using loopholes to avoid taxes (the companies in fact paid less than the affiliates of foreign oil companies) and of withholding and falsifying information concerning access prices paid for crude, in order to keep administered prices unnecessarily high. It accused the two French companies of conspiring with the affiliates of the Majors to maintain the unusually high jet fuel prices supplied to Air France, another state firm. Finally, it accused the state-appointed auditors of representing company interests to the state rather than the reverse.

Although the petroleum industry found, not without some justification, the charges somewhat picayune and

[39] The Schvartz Report is summarized in Le Monde, 8 November 1974. See also note 33 above.

politically motivated, the implications of the report's allegations have a direct bearing on the present discussion.[40] Recalling the exhortations of the Nora Report to spur public enterprise to profit maximization in the international market, a demonstration that French petroleum companies do indeed act like their "competition" should come as no surprise.[41] What is at issue is whether profit maximization in an oligopolistic market tends to push public firms in a direction contradictory to their mandate. That is, profit-maximizing criteria may produce disincentives for achieving goals of supply security and positive balance of payments effects, to say nothing of providing petroleum at reasonable prices. In this sense, the Schvartz Report provides clues not only to the problem but also to the explanation. The charges concerning information about access prices to crude and the role of state auditors have the most important ramifications.

ACCESS PRICES FOR CRUDE

Given the obscure process by which crude prices (not to be confused with the largely fictitious "posted prices") are agreed upon in the world of international oil, it would seem only logical that a state-owned firm—certainly where 100 percent of the equity was held by the state—could provide yeoman's service by enlightening authorities about the real costs of petroleum. This is especially true both because the state has the responsibility to set domestic market petroleum product prices and because petroleum products are used in almost every type of production in a modern economy.

[40] For a detailed reply to the Schvartz Report by the industry trade association, see Union des Chambres Syndicales de l'Industrie Pétrolière, "L'Industrie Française du Pétrole Répond," UCSIP Pamphlet (Paris: UCSIP, December 1974).

[41] S. Nora, *Rapport sur les Entreprises Publiques* (Paris: Documentation Française, 1967). Referred to hereafter as the Nora Report. See also Chapter 1 above.

Many officials and executives interviewed, in fact, prided themselves on this role. One Elf executive stated categorically, "Elf has a majority stockholder, the state. That counts! The importance of Elf Corporation is the possibility of better access to information for the state." Yet an official at the Office of Prices and Competition in the Ministry of Finance was less impressed with Elf's candor, though not unsympathetic to the company's complaints. Noting that "we really can't play the French companies against the international companies," he continued, "of course, we have difficulties with the petroleum firms, even the nationalized ones. It's the same with other enterprises, like EDF. But that's understandable; all these corporations have long-term strategies."[42]

Part of the problem in this regard is not only a desire to maintain commercial secrets, but the fact that actual access prices are extremely complicated and not always easily calculated. This was the chief defense of the industry against the Schvartz Report's claim that the companies had furnished the state with misleading costs. The difficulty in determining the actual cost of access to crude was implicit in the comments of another high-ranking Elf executive when confronted with the Price Office's apparent skepticism: "We give them our costs—access to crude by country—perhaps they [the Price Office] mean that if they had asked us to provide twenty guys to do the calculations and we refused, that I'd understand. We don't have the resources for that."

Clearly, even if the companies were not guilty of the bad faith implied by the Schvartz Report, cost calculations require a level of expertise not readily available to the administration, and thus this expertise becomes a lever by which the industry can fend off administrative encroachment. This, of course, is a familiar problem in govern-

[42] EDF is Electricité de France, the nationalized power company for all of France.

ment-business relations. Not unlike the United States,[43] the French administration depends heavily on the trade association for its information, particularly for statistics. The only petroleum data that the administration receives independently of the industry are those collected by the Customs Office. But the inadequacy of these data to detect discrepancies was admitted by at least one official interviewed. This is not, of course, a situation unique to the oil industry: dependence on trade associations for economic statistics is a fact of life for French administrators. Interestingly, though, none of those interviewed found this dependence particularly disturbing and many insisted on the "excellent quality" of the statistics provided.

In this context the entrance of Elf-ERAP into the industry trade association suggests a conception of the firm that was anything but that of the *franc-tireur* so defended by sympathetic administrators. A key official of UCSIP, the major petroleum trade association, was asked if there was fear of Elf being a Trojan horse. He replied, "No, the French [nationalized] enterprises in a sector are like the others. The relationship between the state and the profession is clear: it is one of consultation."

The attitude of treating the nationalized enterprises "like the others" and as equal rather than subordinate to the state has certainly been reinforced by official policy and pronouncement. Articulated explicitly in the Nora Report which, as one Elf executive remarked, "was even applied here before the letter," and epitomized by Elf president Albin Chalandon's declaration that "I no longer consider that Elf has a public service mission,"[44] the attitude that nationalized firms were *comme les autres* suggests that al-

[43]Cf. Robert Engler, *The Brotherhood of Oil* (Chicago: University of Chicago Press, 1977).

[44]This was widely reported. For the English version see *The Economist*, 23 December 1978, p. 73. Chalandon was rebuked for this remark by André Giraud, minister of industry, who reminded Chalandon that Elf's job was to ensure France's oil supplies.

though the Schvartz Report's allegations of lying about the access prices for crude may have been exaggerated, the incentive to do so was certainly present.

STATE AUDITORS

State auditors (*contrôleurs d'état*) are the official watchdogs of the French government and enjoy considerable statutory authority in the service of their mission as representatives of the state's interests. Their function is much like that of the U.S. General Accounting Office, although the contrôleurs' responsibilities involve only the nationalized firms, unlike the GAO's surveillance of government agencies. One of the defining attributes of a mixed corporation (*société mixte*) like the CFP and an entirely state-owned enterprise like ERAP is that the former has no state audit mission, although it does have state-appointed board members representing supervisory ministries.[45] All participations and joint ventures undertaken by Elf must have the approval of the auditor if the participation does not exceed 50 percent, and requires ministerial approval for majority participations. Unlike any American equivalent, the auditor intervenes periodically during the development of the budget and plan, and occasionally when there are large movements of capital, such as the merger of ERAP with the Société Nationale des Pétroles d'Aquitaine. As a factor in the planning of major corporate strategies, the power of the auditor is considerable. Yet authority and use of authority are not the same. It is significant to consider the response of a member of this mission about his con-

---

[45]The 1976 merger of Elf with the semi-nationalized Société Nationale des Pétroles d'Aquitaine, forming the Société Nationale Elf-Aquitaine (SNEA), resulted in a reduced state share of the equity (70 percent), and "ERAP" became the holding company for the State shares. The holding company remained 100 percent state-owned. Private investors own the other 30 percent of SNEA. Under French law only ERAP's books may be opened to public scrutiny. Thus, the merger was decried as a denationalization of Elf. See Philippe Simonnot, *Le Complot Pétrolier* (Paris: Editions Alain Moreau, 1976).

ception of his role: "We participate at the level of financial authorizations. We don't participate [directly] in the formulation of policy, but we have a function of advice, of counsel, and of information. *The important thing is that the enterprise should be economically profitable.*"[46]

The implication of this is clear. It is a reaffirmation of the sentiment of the Nora Report, and assumes that the company in maximizing its own interests also serves the state. However, there is clearly a structural conflict between the companies and the state over prices which was exaggerated by the 1973–1974 oil crisis. The same official took note of the conflict, making clear where his sympathies lay: "Prices are a source of friction. For us, our function is to defend the viability of the enterprise. It's true that the Ministry of Finance is too sensitive to the [consumer] price index. Since 1973 there has been a real problem with prices."[47]

In this sense there is some justification in the Schvartz Report's concern over the ambiguity of the role of the state audit mission, an ambiguity that clouds the very nature of the nationalized industry in France.

OTHER INSTANCES OF COMPANY-STATE CONFLICT

It is important to consider the conflicts mentioned in the Schvartz Report in a larger context. If it recounts simply a series of isolated incidents, then serious criticism of the organization of the public petroleum sector would be misplaced, especially in light of the positive aspects of these firms discussed earlier. However, the problems seem less anecdotal and more endemic as their number increases. Other incidents indicate that there is a serious problem of

[46] Emphasis added.

[47] It is interesting to note that despite his sympathies with the plight of French oil companies, this interviewee staunchly defended the Schvartz Report. "It is important," he said, "to distinguish the report, which was a good report, from the use made of it by the political parties."

control of public firms, both when the firms become increasingly independent of political authorities, and when they pursue goals—with the blessing of authorities—that are of doubtful benefit to the French economy.

The most interesting cases of company refusal to submit to state orders are, not surprisingly, the most difficult to document. These cases include the refusals by the CFP and Elf to divert oil deliveries from foreign to French customers during the crisis of 1973–1974 and by Elf to renew its cooperation agreement with Algeria in 1975; and their general refusal to implement state-to-state contracts on other than commercial terms. More recently, the companies came into conflict with the state over the Kerr-Magee and Texas Gulf acquisitions in 1980–1981 and over contracts with Mexico in 1981.

The first incident was reported by Robert Stobaugh. Although France was nominally exempt from the 1973 embargo in compensation for official pro-Arab sympathies, the Majors diverted supplies from France to embargoed countries. The government wanted Elf and the CFP to make up the difference:

In spite of all these directives [by the Algerian government to deliver its oil to France] on November 21, 1973 the Majors announced December delivery cuts to France. Although the [French] government had never veered from its original instructions to companies [to maintain scheduled deliveries], the companies, even the two French companies, had never promised to follow them. The only difference between the French and foreign companies, so far as the government was concerned was that it had access to the records of the former, and not of the latter. The CFP allocated its supplies along the same pattern as the Majors. When disagreement arose between the government and CFP, the CFP won the dispute and delivered the oil. Elf-ERAP also continued

77

to deliver oil to its non-French customers, although the amounts were smaller because France had always comprised most of Elf-ERAP's market.[48]

Stobaugh goes on to add that:

During its negotiations with the oil companies the French government shielded the stresses and strains from the French public. Jean Charbonnel, Minister of Science and Industrial Development, sought to allay any fears by announcing in November that France had a 90-day stock of oil and that supplies were coming in normally. He also maintained that the foreign companies were diverting oil from France to other countries where prices were higher, reinforcing the myth that the CFP and Elf-ERAP, being under his direct control, were the salvation of France in the crisis.[49]

Most of those interviewed denied knowledge of the incident, although one CFP executive affirmed that Stobaugh's accusation was "quite possible." What is important to stress, however, is that such behavior casts doubt on the value of a policy encouraging and even subsidizing the extension of French companies' access to crude if that crude cannot be brought back to France in emergencies. Obviously, security of supply becomes meaningless.

The continuation of Elf's commitment to Algeria also appears to be an example of friction between the public firms and the state. Algeria was important to France both for the very good reason that its oil could be paid for in francs and because Algeria was meant to show the Third World the advantages of "special relations" with France.

When it came time to renew the Franco-Algerian cooperation agreement in 1971, negotiations to renew the treaty were conducted for the state by such well-known public

[48] Robert B. Stobaugh, "The Oil Companies in the Crisis" *Daedalus* 104 (Fall 1975), p. 190.
[49] Ibid., p. 191.

servants as François Xavier Ortoli and subsequently by Hervé Alphand. Finally, at an impasse, the state withdrew from the talks in the spring of 1971 and asked the companies to negotiate on their own behalves. Contracts were signed on December 15, 1971, to be renewed in 1975. The contract was not renewed by Elf in 1975, ostensibly for purely commercial reasons, because they judged Algeria's terms for renewal too constricting and too expensive. The CFP did renew its contract, however, which raises questions about other possible motives for Elf's rejection.[50] Certainly, Algerian crude was expensive and Elf did not control the same downstream outlets as the CFP, which could more easily make use of Algeria's "sweet" crude. This low-sulpher crude was best adapted to producing gasoline, which the CFP could distribute internationally and more widely than Elf, since Elf had fewer service stations and served the relatively small French demand for gasoline. Thus, Elf did have good commercial reasons for not renewing its contract. However, these reasons were hardly new. Algerian crude had always been ill-adapted to the French market, yet the position of the French government had always been to maintain a presence in Algeria. State officials apparently viewed *access* to crude as more important than the *kind* of crude one had access to. This was not a view shared by Elf executives. Strangely, negotiators for Elf maintained when interviewed that there had been no government pressure to conclude the contract. One member of the team even insisted that there had been some pressure in the opposite direction by circles in the Foreign Ministry, who preferred another state-to-state contract.[51]

Clearly, even if Elf's refusal to renew the Algerian accord were based only on commercial criteria, that very reason might cast doubt on the value of national champi-

[50] "Bulletin de l'Etranger," *Le Monde*, 15 November 1975.

[51] For a more detailed discussion of the Algerian case, see Jean-Marie Chevalier, *Le Nouvel Enjeu Pétrolier* (Paris: Calmann-Lévy, 1973), pp. 141–172.

ons. France has justified high domestic prices to keep Elf and the CFP viable, yet there was certainly no need for a national champion to be the instrument of state-to-state deals. None of the deals negotiated by the French and foreign-producer governments ever amounted to a very large proportion of French needs (a proposed "maxi-contract" with Saudi Arabia to supply a major portion of French needs over a twenty-year period never materialized),[52] but the deals that were negotiated were sufficiently lucrative to bring complaints from the private companies that were excluded. One executive of a French affiliate of a Major informed me that his company had complained when they were refused participation in the Saudi contract, and another reminded me that "we are French, too!" In fact, a ranking executive of Elf made it very clear that commercial (that is, highly profitable) terms were the *only* terms, and that the company would accede to French government demands only if it were worth its while: "When the state negotiates a contract with an OPEC country, it's because that country wants a higher price. . . . If the state wants us to negotiate a contract for political reasons, we say, 'You pay for it!' "[53] Presumably, on these terms any corporation (even a multinational) might fulfill—indeed eagerly—the function of a national champion.

WHY NOT AN ELF-CFP MERGER?

Other actions point up the contradictions in French oil policy. For instance, the state has encouraged Elf's exploration in the North Sea although Great Britain has categorically refused to allow Elf to export its North Sea crude to France. Thus, it would seem at first glance that the effect of state policy has been to subsidize British security of supply, in the sense that high oil prices on the French

[52] *Financial Times* (London), 9 January 1974.

[53] The Saudi contract quoted crude at 93 percent of the posted price (standard commercial terms) which was termed "advantageous" in *Les Echos* (Paris), 28 January 1977.

domestic market represented a subsidy from consumers to the companies that in turn supplied the British market. However, officials interviewed justify the North Sea investment not in terms of security of supply, but in terms of increasing Elf's size by increasing its cash flow, the cash coming from the sale of Elf's North Sea oil to British customers. This is an instance of the argument that French companies are not yet large enough to take on the Majors in defense of French interests. It is intriguing that the officials interviewed who offered this explanation refused to consider merging Elf and the CFP.

In a rare interview in 1973, Elf president Guillaumat, a formidable figure in French politics, implied that the merger was opposed by then President Pompidou, although Guillaumat's his own opposition to the plan was well known.[54] This was ostensibly because such a firm would be "too big to manage," a rationale echoed by high-ranking executives interviewed at the CFP. One suspects that such a complaint does not reverberate in the board room of Exxon or Mobil.

Clearly, the pinnacles of authority in the two French firms would run the risk of losing ground in the new hierarchy resulting from an eventual merger, not to mention a loss of jobs for the *Corps de Mines*. Yet the reluctance to pursue the seeming logic of competitive size does not only emanate from the firms involved. The administration is also hesitant to create a potential rival center of power. As one official close to Giscard d'Estaing put it quite candidly: "Politically, it would be difficult for the state to take a majority share of the CFP. Moreover, we'd be afraid of the political power of the president of a group resulting from a merger of Elf and the CFP."

As is so often overlooked by economists, size has political effects and thus political limits. The paradoxical result in the case of French petroleum policy is that the policy

---

[54] *Nouvel Observateur,* 12 February 1973, p. 78.

set by politicians implies an optimum that is proscribed by the same politicians.

A RESURGENCE OF CONTROL?

It should be noted that there has been movement on the part of the state to reestablish some control over its two petroleum firms, but the very clashes that triggered the control mechanisms indicate a continued divergence of interests between companies pursuing strategies of profit maximization and the stewards of the public interest.

One would expect, after the publication of the Schvartz Report at the end of 1974, that the state would feel itself under some pressure to demonstrate itself the master of the situation. Oddly enough, this did not happen; no real incidents of conflict arose between 1975 and 1979. Reasons for this period of acquiescence can be inferred.

The first and probably most convincing reason is that the petroleum supply situation had largely settled down in the period. Although the impact of the post-1973 price increases was still being felt in the form of rampant inflation, the lack of supply disruption tended to allow public attention to be diverted from the problems of energy dependence. The bureaucracy had adjusted prices to account for the increased cost of crude, and the downward pressure on prices from the Rotterdam spot market was a relatively minor thorn in the side of the industry. Although excess refining capacity and obsolete equipment were particular problems of the French petroleum industry, these were also relatively minor when compared with the catastrophic situation of the French steel and textile sectors.

The political situation also facilitated the acquiescence. With legislative elections not scheduled until 1978, the government had a breathing spell and the opposition had turned its attention to internal fence-mending. In that the Left's common platform of 1972 projected a wave of nationalizations (which in fact occurred in 1982), the Left had a low incentive to pursue a campaign based on the flaws of nationalized industries. Since the major problem was inflation, the sources of this economic malady could be viewed as diffuse and systemic, rather than looking for individual perpetrators. Nevertheless, conflict with the public sector did occur and some—perhaps minor—victories by the state suggest that the lack of control of public enterprise that forms the theme of this chapter is not totally inherent in the French administrative apparatus.

The first point to mention in this regard is the renewed pressure on the state resulting from the second oil price explosion in 1979. The ability of the administration to resist industry demands for the elimination of price controls (see Chapter 2) suggests both some residue of state power and a willingness to use it.

Other evidence suggests this same conclusion. Elf, for instance, prepared a takeover bid for the American firm Kerr-Magee in 1980. Raymond Barre, then prime minister, personally axed the plan only hours before it was to take effect—ostensibly for diplomatic reasons, given France's fragile relations with the United States.[55] More importantly, perhaps, the Ministry of Industry opposed the use of Elf's cash flow for buying known supplies of crude (that is, the holdings of Kerr-Magee) and nonpetroleum sources of energy (France has considerable reserves of uranium, Kerr-Magee's other attraction) when the money could be used for oil exploration.[56] Although the state prevailed in this instance, it points out another problem of managerial autonomy: managers tend to be risk-averse while benefiting from state support meant to subsidize risk. Thus Chalandon's strategy was to shift Elf's holdings to North America and out of oil. This may be prudent management for a goal of preserving and augmenting cash flow, but it does nothing to augment France's oil supply security. True enough, North American oil is not controlled by volatile

[55] *New York Times,* 22 November 1981.
[56] *Le Monde,* 18 July 1980.

sheiks, but the French companies, after all, did not favor diverting deliveries from foreign clients any more than the American Majors during the last world oil shortage. France indeed would be no less secure, given Elf's previous performance, if Kerr-Magee remained in American hands. Yet the fact that the government denied Elf its North American strategy suggests precisely a reassertion of control that made Elf's actions logical from the point of view of the public interest. If the government *could* direct Elf's activities, acquisition of Kerr-Magee made sense. This logic suggests that the government's denial of the Kerr-Magee acquisition had more to do with the well-known personal animosity between the Minister of Industry and the president of Elf and their conflicting loyalties than with the merits of the acquisition, or a reassertion of the public interest.[57]

The subsequent decision in 1982 to allow Elf's acquisition of Texasgulf, a diversified mineral corporation in the United States,[58] also suggests that the original Kerr-Magee deal was stymied for reasons of elite conflict. The new minister of industry, Pierre Dreyfus, was much more sympathetic to Chalandon, having been president of a public firm himself (Renault), and was personally committed to the principle of an independent management. The permission to acquire Texasgulf led many in the French company to breathe a sign of relief. The Socialists could, after all, have urged that Elf's profits be used to buy up failing French companies in order to preserve employment. Indeed, the fact that these fears were voiced by Elf's executives underlines the fact that the state can do just that.[59] The decision by Socialist officials to allow Elf to use normal corporate criteria in the allocation of its profits only serves to emphasize the continuity of Socialist policy towards public enterprise with respect to previous regimes. We will return to this theme in the last chapter. Suffice it

[57] See Chapter 4.
[58] *New York Times*, 22 November 1981.
[59] Ibid.

to conclude the point here with a quote from the comments of an Elf executive committee member: "We want to be viewed as serious business people."[60]

The red flags are more likely to show, however, when company decisions run overtly counter to the government's foreign policy. Such was the case in the CFP's termination of its Mexican contract in July of 1981.[61] Suffering from a surfeit of petroleum, the semi-private company decided to abrogate its contract (legally) for expensive Mexican oil. The company pursued this course despite considerable arm-twisting from the Socialists, who were anxious to maintain close ties with Mexico for a variety of reasons.[62] The government finally succeeded in getting the CFP to renew its crude purchases, but only after the Mexican government broke off all economic relations with France. It is not clear whether it was the extremity of the retaliation or a government deal with the CFP that led CFP managers to return to the Mexican well, but the implications are clear and reiterate the themes of this study. Firms pursuing microeconomic profit incentives are likely to come into conflict with the macroeconomic concerns of the state. For this reason the goals established for a nationalized sector cannot be identical to those for the private sector. The reluctance or inability of a state to impose such goals has important implications: there is either some weakness in the state that prevents it from imposing the public interest on the private sector, or the state itself is simply the appendage of some interest or coalition of interests.

Conclusion

We noted in Chapter 2 that French domestic market regulation, like the American variety, has been in the in-

[60] Ibid.

[61] Le Monde, 8 July 1981.

[62] This was recounted to me by a journalist from Le Monde. I did not obtain independent verification of the government's arm-twisting before Mexico's retaliation.

terests of those regulated. It appears that the value of the national champion firms as instruments of the commonwealth is also suspect, especially as interests of the state and its appendages diverge. Added to this is the fact that the national champions are publicly owned while colluding with private interests. Thus, controlling these public enterprises leads us to focus again on the ambiguous frontiers of state and society. But first a closer look at the French state is in order. This time we must examine the processes by which state policies are produced.

CHAPTER FOUR

The Policy Process

> On a commission like this it doesn't pay to have imagination.
>
> member of the French Nuclear
> Advisory Commission

Who is responsible for policy? What elements constrain choice? By what process are alternatives chosen? These are essential considerations if one is to understand the strengths and deficiencies of French economic policy in general and petroleum policy in particular. Obstacles to control are real, basic, and far from random. The French system of elite recruitment, administrative organization, and policy choice all combine to hinder pursuit of a rational and coherent public petroleum policy.

Who Makes Policy?

It has become commonplace to remark on the primacy of the French administration in both the creation and implementation of public policy. The demise of legislatures as centers for the formulation of policy is, of course, a well-documented reality of the twentieth century, and the decline of parliamentary influence on policy decisions is nowhere more obvious than in France.[1] Certainly since 1958, the architecture of the Palais Bourbon, home of the French National Assembly, has not included corridors of

[1] Reasons for this range from the growth of party discipline (e.g., in the U.K.), to the need in all countries for a strong executive to promote coherent government economic intervention, to simply the preferences of charismatic figures (such as de Gaulle in France). Work on this question is too voluminous to provide specific references here.

power. The President's Elysée Palace and the prime minister's Hôtel Matignon are much more accommodating in this regard, as are the relevant bureaucracies under their supervision.

Responsibility for petroleum policy within the administration falls to a number of ministries and agencies. Among them are principally the Ministries of Industry, Finance, and Foreign Affairs, and the executive offices of the President and prime minister. More marginally, the Council of State (Conseil d'Etat) and the Court of Accounts (Cour des Comptes) exercise legal controls that limit the range of choices available to officials.

THE MINISTRY OF INDUSTRY

The Ministry of Industry is both the primary supervisory ministry (*ministère de tutelle*) of the national oil companies (Elf and CFP) and, with the exception of domestic pricing which was transferred to the Ministry of Finance in 1976 and then to the Ministry of the Economy when Finance was split in 1978, the Ministry of Industry is also the chief regulatory authority of the petroleum sector. The petroleum interests of the Ministry of Industry are in turn supervised through its Oil and Gas Department (formerly DICA, the Office of Motor Fuels, which in turn was successor to the National Liquid Fuel Office created in 1925). This department serves both as the conduit of policy imperatives to the industry and as the repository of technical advice to the government.[2] It is here that accordance of import licenses is decided, based on predictions of French market needs, as well as other related licensing matters (e.g., new refineries, distribution points).[3] Contact with the industry is not simply periodic, as this licensing procedure would imply, but continuous both because DICA of-

[2] The sophistication of this technical role will be examined below. I have retained use of the acronym DICA for simplicity.

[3] Farid Saad, "France and Oil: A Contemporary Economic Study," Ph.D. diss., M.I.T., 1969, pp. 32ff. The quota system was reformed in 1978.

ficials sit on national company boards, and because they continually consult on government-subsidized projects (e.g., technical research), have approximately weekly pricing meetings, and have a general technical role in the determination of long-range policy.

The Ministry of Industry is linked to broader policy considerations both through the Délégué Général à l'Energie (renamed Minister of Energy under Mitterrand and though formerly an agent of the prime minister, now attached directly to the Ministry of Industry as a junior minister), and through the interministerial supervisory committees that coordinate policy for national companies.[4] This is, of course, in addition to the minister of industry's participation in the government.

THE MINISTRY OF FINANCE

Structurally opposed to the Ministry of Industry, a spending ministry,[5] is the Ministry of Finance, the awesome ministry whose job it is "to say no." Its massive presence and labyrinthine corridors in the Palais du Louvre contain the machinery that considers policy against the criteria of state priorities expressed in financial terms. Most directly concerned with energy policies and particularly with public firms are the Offices of the Budget and of the Treasury. The former pays special attention to the impact of public spending (via nationalized firms and industry subsidies) on broader goals; the latter regards with a jaundiced eye state interventions and company actions that may substantially affect the money supply. In this vein both offices collaborate with the state audit missions in nation-

[4]The director of the DICA reported to the Délégué Général under Giscard. *Délégué Général*, or General Delegate, is a term that signifies interministerial responsibilities in French administrative usage. The post was renamed Minister of Energy by Mitterrand, but it was unclear whether this junior minister was given any real authority.

[5]Cf. Guy Lord, *The French Budgetary Process* (Berkeley and Los Angeles: University of Califronia Press, 1973), pp. 45ff.

alized firms and take part, through the minister of finance, in broader policy debates.

THE MINISTRY OF FINANCE AND THE ECONOMY

After the 1978 legislative elections, the Ministry of Finance and the Economy was truncated, ostensibly, to ensure a more optimum division of labor. Signs on buildings were dutifully changed and the Bureau of Prices, newly named the Office of Prices and Competition (Direction de la Concurrence et des Prix) in honor of Giscard's commitment to less *dirigisme*, continued its functions as the chief agency responsible for domestic petroleum prices. This did not change when the ministries were recombined under Mitterrand. Although restrictions on some products, namely heavy fuel oil and naphtha, have been relaxed, this agency has the complicated task of determining the prices French consumers will pay for petroleum-based energy. That is to say, it has responsibility for technical preparation of pricing decisions. Ultimately, as noted in Chapter 2, price responsibility lies with Matignon and the Elysée. This system was somewhat modified in 1982 and will be discussed in Chapter 6.

THE MINISTRY OF FOREIGN AFFAIRS

The Ministry of Foreign Affairs has the most intermittent role in the formulation of energy policy. Although represented formally and informally in the administrative structure of the national companies,[6] its role has been more than consultative only during attempts to negotiate state-to-state contracts. Even then, public servants who enjoyed independent prestige, such as Hervé Alphand and Hugue de l'Estoile, played roles eclipsing officials more closely tied to the ministry.[7]

[6] For example, Philippe Labouret, second in charge at the CFP, was a foreign service officer before joining the company.

[7] Hugue de l'Estoile, motivating force behind the Saudi contract, later joined the partially nationalized Dassault aviation company.

INTERMINISTERIAL RESPONSIBILITIES

Since policy options affect elements of the administration differently, conflicts are often worked out in a number of interministerial forums. Ultimately, of course, responsibility resides with the President, but as might be expected and according to those interviewed, presidential intervention occurs only when decisions substantially affect the overall price level or if they affect foreign policy. Even the intervention of the prime minister, who is basically in charge of day-to-day management of governmental affairs in the hybrid regime established by the 1958 constitution, is rather limited. One high-ranking official of unusual longevity in energy affairs carefully remarked that he "could only recall perhaps ten times when the prime minister intervened" during this official's tenure of over three decades in petroleum affairs.

Under Giscard, the Délégué Général à l'Energie was largely responsible for arbitrating conflicts among different agencies. However, most policy regarding national companies is worked out in the supervisory "Special Committee," where relevant agencies are represented.

Parliament only seems to enter the process by its almost *pro forma* approval of the budget. For this reason it is represented on the Petroleum Advisory Council (Conseil Supérieur du Pétrole). The importance of this council as a decision-making forum was uniformly discounted by members of the administration and company executives who were interviewed for this study. Although all the principal agencies, company representatives, and interested members of Parliament—particularly the chairman of the Finance Commission—are represented in the council, bureaucrats and company executives were consistent in maintaining that its function was one of disseminating information.

The final outpost of interministerial coordination is the Planning Commission (Commissariat Général du Plan). Far from its halcyon days, the Planning Commission under Giscard wielded very little of the power or prestige that earned it kudos as the model for modern capitalism. In the decades after World War II, the Planning Commission was the hub of public and private sector collaboration to co-ordinate investments and avoid production bottlenecks.[8] Because of Giscard's ideological commitment to economic liberalism and because the open French economy was increasingly vulnerable to unplannable developments in the world market, the Planning Commission's influence became limited to giving advice on priority projects, a special budgetary category absorbing about 15 percent of the state budget, and to a more general role as "technical advisor"[9] to the prime minister when the latter was called upon to arbitrate an interagency dispute. The Mitterrand government restored much prestige to the Plan and its general evolution will be more carefully examined below.

Although the preceding organizations constitute the essential roster of participants in the continuous process of policy formulation, certain groups also contribute, albeit irregularly, to the formulation of petroleum policy. It is here that Parliament plays a more significant role. As in any western industrial society, budgets must be submitted to Parliament. Even the emasculated National Assembly of the Fifth Republic holds at least nominal power in this regard and its potential at least to obstruct administration-conceived policy is considerable. With the notable, although temporary, exception of the Assembly's initial rejection of the budget in 1979, this power has been essentially academic in the past as parties allied to the President have dominated the legislature. This was no less true under the Left after 1981 than during the first twenty years of the

---

[8] Andrew Shonfield, *Modern Capitalism* (New York: Oxford University Press, 1969); chaps. 4,5,7; see also Stephen S. Cohen, *Modern Capitalist Planning: The French Model* (Berkeley and Los Angeles: University of California Press, 1977).

[9] This was the term used by one of the persons interviewed.

Fifth Republic. Nevertheless, pains are taken to accommodate or at least to inform important committee members on petroleum matters, especially the chairman of the Finance Commission. In addition, Parliament's capacity to form ad hoc committees in particular areas has most notably accrued influence to members of the Ad Hoc Committee on Petroleum Industries (Schvartz Commission) and, less sensationally, to members of the Commission of Inquiry into Nationalized Industry (Bonnefous Commission). The reports of both of these commissions seemed to have little impact other than to make administrative agencies even more secretive.[10]

LEGAL CONTROL

One needs to take note of another set of occasional actors in the policy process, specifically the Council of State and the Court of Accounts. By law, responsibility for scrutiny of nationalized industry falls to the Public Enterprise Accountability Commission (Commission de Verification des Entreprises Publiques), a court constituted essentially of members of the elite Court of Accounts. Although this is all too often a rather *pro forma* affair, it nevertheless provides a structure for routine audits of the public sector. Because of differing corporate charters, the CFP, a mixed ownership corporation (*société mixte*), does not undergo as extensive a state scrutiny as Elf, a state corporation (*société d'état*).

The Council of State supervises the French system of administrative courts. Here complaints of procedural or substantive maladministration are heard and ruled upon. The role is particularly important for allocation of import licenses. The DICA decisions on the quantities of crude it

[10]When I asked the DICA for a time series of company profit figures, a simple request in the United States, they declined saying the "U.S. companies don't have Schvartz Report to deal with." This kind of information is not clearly indicated by corporate annual reports, given French companies' heralded penchant for intentionally vague bookkeeping.

will allow each company to import (A-3 and A-10 authorizations) are subject to appeal before the Council of State. As was noted in Chapter 2, any cartel where prices are fixed creates an incentive for participants to jockey for the maximum possible share in order to maximize profits. Thus charges of discrimination in the allocation of quotas are not uncommon, although the overall benefits of French market regulation keep discontent within bounds.[11] In this context the Council of State provides acceptable machinery for "arbitration" of disputes among cartel partners.

THE COMPANIES AS PARTICIPANTS IN POLICY FORMULATION

Essentially autonomous, public and private petroleum companies are responsible for the framework that shapes the options available to government. Both by omission and by design, French and foreign-based companies enjoy considerable freedom of action. As one interviewee remarked when asked to define French petroleum policy, "The state has no policy: it leaves everything to the companies!"

Certainly there has been in France, as in most western countries, a remarkable coincidence between the policy objectives of public officials and the broad interests of the petroleum industry, whether this involves the primacy of supply considerations or, more mundanely, preserving the advantages that have accrued to companies in a protected market. Companies are both, as we shall see, the main repositories of expertise and active promoters of policies that administrators are all too inclined to accept.

[11] A-3 and A-10 are three- and ten-year import authorizations. Cf. Saad, "France and Oil," p. 38. At the time I was conducting my research, Mobil was charging discrimination. Shell and Exxon also expressed concern, but this was directed at French company requests for state aid to refining during the European petroleum glut preceding the 1978–1979 Iranian crisis. The French national companies were hit much harder than the affiliates of the Majors.

Problems of Control

COMMISSAIRES AND STATE AUDITORS

Government policy is most directly represented by the government commissioners (*commissaires du gouvernement*) and the state auditors. The duty of the commissioner is to represent the technical minister (usually the Ministries of Industry and Foreign Affairs) and to exercise "control" of particular, as opposed to general, activities of the companies such as individual investments or diversification decisions. The commissioner is the state's representative on the corporate board (*conseil d'administration*), ostensibly to ensure that company policy decisions will not transgress upon larger state objectives. Formally, this amounts to a veto over both the CFP and Elf. In reality, the attempt to assert this power occurred only once in the memory of the officials interviewed. This rarity can be deceiving, however, for the formal decision of a commissioner as with that of an auditor, takes place after a considerable period of informal bargaining through which the interests and opinions of various supervisory agencies are taken into account. This was the case, for example, when Elf wished to invest in a U.S. petrochemical firm. The Office of the Treasury made it known, informally, that it would approve such an investment only if the acquired firm were to open a branch in France to create employment opportunities for the depressed southwest region of the country. The Elf executives agreed and incorporated this into the investment proposal subsequently approved by its government commissioner and state auditor.

The state auditor is in charge of supervising the economic and financial activity of a public enterprise and reports to the Ministry of Finance. What makes this particular position interesting from our point of view is its essential ambiguity. Writing in general terms, one student of French law in the matter has observed:

The office is normally entrusted to senior officials, but their functions are not really defined. No one is charged with coordinating the instructions they receive, their activities are not supervised and are scarcely controlled at all. . . . The *Contrôleurs d'Etat* are essentially concerned with supervising the economic and financial activity of the enterprise but each *contrôleur* has a particular understanding of his own task. Some of them are concerned above all, and almost exclusively, with an examination of an entirely formal character; others, on the contrary, occupy themselves with problems of administration and of economic decisions. Yet others appear, after considerable time passed, as if they were in fact *representatives of the enterprise and have a tendency to take on the defense rather than act as true controllers.*[12]

Interestingly, the time needed for an auditor to identify with the interests of the enterprise need not be very long, if the auditor interviewed in Chapter 3 is any indication. This member of the state audit mission assumed his post after publication of the Schvartz Report, which accused his predecessor of similar identification. The comments quoted in Chapter 3 are testimony to his own identification with company interests.

DOMINATION OF THE POLICY PROCESS

We have now only a partial picture of policy formulation and implementation. As Weber noted, "The essential question is always: who dominates the bureaucratic machinery?"[13] An answer to this question requires that it be taken in two ways. Does a particular post in the bureau-

---

[12]D.M.G. Lévy, "Control of Public Enterprise in France," in *Government Enterprise*, ed. W. Friedmann and J. F. Garner, and trans. J. F. Garner (London: Stevens and Sons, 1970), p. 129. Emphasis added.

[13]Quoted in Max Rheinstein, ed., *Max Weber on Law in Economy and Society*, trans. Edward Shils and Max Rheinstein (New York: Simon and Schuster, 1967), p. xxxiv.

cracy necessarily carry more leverage than others because of the nature of the post? Or are some individuals more influential regardless of the post they occupy?

FORMAL LEVERAGE

Some posts in the bureaucracy offer intrinsically powerful levers of influence. These are not only positions that are *hierarchically* closest to the locus of decision making, but also posts where the assigned task in the bureaucratic division of labor is inherently more influential in the policy process. Such is the case of the Ministry of Finance when compared with the influence of the technical ministries, even though technical ministers hold the same legal status as the Finance minister in the administrative hierarchy. Control of the purse strings is what makes the administrators of the Finance Ministry more awesome than those of the Ministry of Industry.

The intrinsic power of the Ministry of Finance is tempered, however, in several ways. First, by its own division of labor, suboffices within the ministry have conflicting interests regarding policy recommendations. As remarked earlier, the Budget and Treasury Offices have separate concerns and tend to emphasize those policies that will have a more minimal impact on their respective bailiwicks. Thus the Treasury Office pushes for company support to be drawn from state subsidies rather than risk a drain on France's shallow capital market, while the Budget Office prefers to minimize subsidies and additional claims on budgetary resources. Both offices have an interest in supporting French petroleum firms through high domestic prices, but here they run into the government's anti-inflationary policies as enforced by the Office of Prices and Competition. Nevertheless, the Ministry of Finance is the *primus inter pares*, its minister generally being the most important political figure after the prime minister.[14]

[14] At the time of most of my interviews both posts were held by Raymond Barre. Giscard d'Estaing's catapult into the country's highest of-

More specific to the case of oil, the sector's immense capacity to draw on external sources of financing limits the power of the official purse. Although the national companies' degree of external indebtedness—more than twice that of the Majors—has been a matter of concern, the fact that they were able to borrow the money they needed gives some indication of the leeway the firms have.[15] This is a state of affairs that has to some degree been encouraged by the Ministry of Finance. It would prefer that the companies use foreign branches to borrow abroad and thus minimize the effect of the loan on the French balance of payments.[16]

If control of the purse is the Finance Ministry's bureaucratic advantage, expertise is the source of leverage for the Ministry of Industry. Members of the Oil and Gas Department (DICA) are awarded their posts partially in recognition of their technical training at the Ecole Polytechnique and the Ecole des Mines, and certainly in recognition of their membership in technical Grands Corps, that is, the groups in France's civil service elite with at least nominally technical functions.[17]

This technical leverage is much more apparent than real. Training at these elite schools consists mainly of short sojourns in industry (stages), which are supposed to give "real world" experience, rather than extensive classroom theory. The result is usually a kind of potpourri of experience that gives the potential civil servant adaptability to a multiplicity of industrial situations. Thus, the "technical" school

---

fice was also the Ministry of Finance. Mitterrand's appointment of moderate Jacques Delors to the post was applauded by the French business community.

[15] *Le Matin de Paris,* 18 November 1977.

[16] Interview with an Elf executive.

[17] The role of the Grands Corps is most carefully examined in Ezra N. Suleiman, *Elites in French Society* (Princeton: Princeton University Press, 1978). It is more briefly treated in his *Politics, Power, and Bureaucracy* (Princeton: Princeton University Press, 1974), chap. 10.

in reality trains generalists who, in a sense, pride themselves on their technical ignorance. Said one member of a Grands Corps in a position of influence, "The education I had gave me no ideas, and hence no preconceived ideas, about the science of management. If I have a few today, they can only be the fruits of a pure autodidacticism."[18] During the period in which interviews were conducted for this study, for example, the new director of the DICA was transferred from a position unrelated to petroleum or the oil industry.

The lack of technical knowledge has the effect of increasing the dependence of the Ministry of Industry upon industry professionals, reinforcing the classic symbiotic relationship between the primary supervisory ministry and its client sector. The essence of this situation, from the perspective of formal bureaucratic leverage, is the structural opposition of the Ministry of Finance, charged with safeguarding the public purse and limiting the impact of inflation, against the tandem of the Ministry of Industry and its client sector.[19]

Naturally, the formal powers of the President and prime minister need not be minimized, for the buck—or franc—stops there. What is important to note, however, in terms of structural influence, is that their interventions are infrequent and the organization of their staffs is even less amenable to producing technically competent counterproposals to the alternatives that percolate up from the bureaucracy. This is mainly because their chief advisors have broadly defined responsibilities, covering vast areas of economic policy. The prime minister has, for instance, one chief advisor for economic affairs, whose staff cannot

[18]Quoted in Ezra N. Suleiman, "The Myth of Technical Expertise: Selection, Organization and Leadership," *Comparative Politics* 10 (October 1977), p. 146. Too great a specialization may lead to remaining in the same job, rather than moving on to bigger and better things.

[19]This problem was also alluded to by interviewees in the Ministry of Finance.

match the detailed coverage available to competing policy sources. A similar situation exists for the President. There are also a conscious effort on the part of the Giscard Administration to downplay the importance of technical expertise in favor of more general political savvy,[20] an effort continued by Mitterrand but mitigated by the latter's vulnerability to charges of cronyism in the management of nationalized industry.

The bias in the French administration toward generalists, then, seems to have two important consequences for the formulation of petroleum policy. First, there is little room for counter-expertise when *any* expertise is in short supply. This is a situation often decried by American policy analysts such as Destler and George with regard to U.S. policy making and has more recently been taken up in France by Simonnot.[21] This lack of counter-expertise is hardly accidental.

The second implication, essentially a corollary of the first, of French reliance upon generalists is an ensuing dependence upon the expertise furnished by the companies. One official interviewed, when confronted with the criticism that the state had no independent sources of information in petroleum affairs, simply shrugged and replied, "It's the same problem for *every* sector in France."

This does not, of course, mean that there is no policy debate in France. At the time most of the interviews were being conducted, there was intense discussion about the degree to which petroleum policy should be "liberalized,"—that is, made more sensitive to "market forces,"

[20] Henry W. Ehrmann, *Politics in France,* 3rd ed. (Boston: Little, Brown, 1976), p. 275.

[21] I. M. Destler, *Presidents, Bureaucrats, and Foreign Policy: The Politics of Organizational Reform* (Princeton: Princeton University Press, 1974); Alexander L. George, *Presidential Decisionmaking in Foreign Policy: The Effective Use of Information and Advice* (Boulder, Co.: Westview Press, 1980), chap. 11; Philippe Simonnot, *Les Nucléocrates* (Grenoble: Presses Universitaires de Grenoble, 1978).

especially with regard to removing price controls on specific products. (In fact, the liberalization of naphtha and fuel oil pricing was a direct result of the recommendations of a private consulting firm.)[22] But although there is debate, it takes place within limits that are defined by a common terminology and a set of shared assumptions: both an understandable acceptance of general rules of the game and an unquestioned faith, even among socialists, in marginalist economic theory. These are limits that are also closely related to the general characteristics of elite cohesion in France.

Elites and the Policy Process

ELITE COHESION: RECRUITMENT

It is no accident that the policy debate in France is narrowly defined. Perhaps no other political elite so enjoys the uniformity of shared perceptions that is characteristic of the French decision-making structure. The upper reaches of the French administration are populated by professional civil servants bound together by a powerful network of formal and informal ties. These are ties that are essentially a product of French education grafted onto a particular form of organization, the Grands Corps.[23]

France's system of education creates distinct channels of elite recruitment through its "specialized" Grandes Ecoles, especially the Ecole Polytechnique, including its Ecole des Mines graduate school, and the Ecole Nationale d'Administration (ENA).[24] The schools provide a pool of candi-

[22] The Arthur Little Company. Their report is still confidential.

[23] These corporate bodies enjoy legal status. For a case study of a single corps see Jean-Claude Thoenig, *L'Ere des Technocrates: Le Cas des Ponts et Chausées* (Paris: Editions d'Organisation, 1973). For the corps generally, see Suleiman, *Elites in French Society.*

[24] The top 10 percent of Polytechnique's graduating class are invited to attend the Ecole des Mines. Polytechnique is the premier engineering school in France and dates back to Napoleon. The Ecole Nationale d'Ad-

dates for France's most prestigious, powerful, and remunerative posts.

Entrance to these schools, part of the Napoleonic heritage and specifically created to provide the state with technically competent personnel, is by competitive examination. And not unlike most countries employing competitive examinations, there is a distinct bias in the process in favor of already-privileged socioeconomic groups.[25] This, of course, only provides a foundation for highly developed elite cohesion. Once in the schools, a long-developed process of reasoning begun in the *lycée* is refined. Unlike the university system, the Grandes Ecoles are not troubled by a diversity of doctrine. Partly because the great measure of courses are taught by active civil servants rather than academics (especially in the ENA) and partly because the intellectual proclivities of the students have been controlled by the entrance examinations and by self-selection, student acceptance of established procedure and orthodoxy is the norm.[26]

Three important consequences need emphasis. The rigid channels of elite recruitment represented by the Grandes Ecoles result in: (1) a highly restrictive and homogeneous pool of elites from which to populate the most crucial centers of decision in French society; (2) an assured transmission of policy orthodoxy, passed on to those most amenable to accepting it; and (3) a common set of school experiences that binds each generation of elites and unites different generations through "old school ties."

Thus the system of elite recruitment creates an administrative edifice greatly biased against policy innovation,

---

ministration was established in 1945 to provide a centralized pool from which to staff the highest reaches of the bureaucracy.

[25] See Suleiman, *Politics, Power, and Bureaucracy*, chaps. 2, 3, and 4.

[26] There are, of course, exceptions. A mini-revolt against the Grande Ecole examination process and the method of recruitment into the Grands Corps took place by members of the ENA graduating class of 1970, who had entered in 1968. They were, however, only a brief aberration.

either because people with alternative conceptions of public policy are not likely to penetrate to the inner circles of decision, or because those who do enter the elite become socialized into accepting existing doctrine well before arriving at positions of power. It is therefore not surprising that French petroleum policy has been both consistent and essentially conservative for more than half a century.

DIVISION AND COHESION: THE GRANDS CORPS

"The Grands Corps are like your American fraternities; they give us a chance to get to know a man, to judge his worth and help us decide if he's the right man for the job." So replied one interviewee, highly influential in French energy policy and long known for his defense of the Grands Corps system. Although not unique to France, this particular form of bureaucratic organization has important repercussions on the formulation of French energy policy.[27]

The Grands Corps are highly institutionalized and self-regulating groups of civil servants organized on a functional basis. Thus one finds, for example, the Corps of Civil Engineers (Corps des Ponts et Chaussées), Inspectors of Finance, Civil Administrators, Foreign Service, and Mining Engineers. These corps take on more administrative importance largely for two reasons: first, they provide personnel to both public and private sectors far beyond the original definitions of their scope of expertise and second, their ability to attract the ablest graduates of the Grandes Ecoles is largely a function of the corps' performance in providing prestigious and powerful posts in the French state and society, leading to considerable competition among the corps.[28]

The Grands Corps' provision of personnel to posts largely outside their original purview (such as mining engineers

[27] Spain also has such a system.
[28] A detailed examination of this phenomenon goes beyond the scope of this study. The interested reader should refer to Suleiman, *Elites in French Society.*

103

to DICA and oil companies and finance inspectors to trade associations) is the result of French administrative largesse. Civil servants are easily granted leaves of absense, often permanent, from their official corps duties, and the practice of slipping from public to private sectors (*pantouflage*) is not only permitted, but encouraged. In fact, a corps member who remains in his official corps function is considered a *raté*, a failure.[29]

Essentially, it is this liberal leave-taking policy that allowed the various corps to adapt to changing circumstances as their old jobs became obsolete or diminished in importance. This, of course, undermined their original raison d'être of functional specialization, in favor of the skills of the generalist. Thus professional dilettantism, known as "*polyvalence*," became the new, sought-after quality.

Nor has this kind of role expansion taken place in a vacuum. No longer barred from positions on the basis of professional education, the corps began to compete with each other to obtain more and more posts for their members. Since function or training was no longer a prerequisite for a post (remembering the premium placed on nonspecialization), competition among the corps reinforced this tendency toward generalism as each of these corporate bodies sought to capture more posts in greater areas of the economy, a phenomenon Suleiman has called "imperialism."[30]

The twin phenomena of corps dilettantism and imperialism have several implications for French petroleum policy. Since expertise must be acquired on the job, there is a bias in favor of producer groups over regulating authorities. Officials remain in state service only to ensure the best possible opportunity for transferring to nationalized or private industry. This means that regulatory authorities are those who have not yet had a chance to *pantoufler*. They

[29] Suleiman, *Elites in French Society*, p. 175.
[30] Ibid., pp. 210ff.

are relatively young, relatively new at their jobs, and not anxious to alienate a prospective employer. As one committee staffer from the National Assembly put it, "The Director of the DICA is usually a civil servant about thirty-five to forty-five years old who has to confront the great companies and their presidents who exercise influence at the level of the Minister."

This, of course, is less a problem where there is horizontal (e.g., Ministry of Finance) rather than vertical (*ministère de tutelle*) control. The conflict of interest is less obvious where the possibilities for *pantouflage* are less direct. However, the average official is at his post for only a few years, and rapid job rotations still decrease expertise on the side of the regulator and in favor of the regulated. Compare this to careers in the petroleum industry, which are characterized—unlike most French industries—by long company service before being accorded significant decision-making responsibility.[31] To compound this disparity of expertise and influence, regulatory teams in the Ministry of Industry tend to be small with very little in the way of permanent funds to study the problems of the industry.[32]

The corollary to this imbalance between regulator and regulated is that what expertise does exist is acquired from company service, and it is not surprising that "informed opinion" reflects the company point of view.

POLICY DISPUTES AND CORPS COMPETITION

Policy conflicts do exist, but they are not the conflicts based on the firm ground of counter-expertise. This is another consequence of Grands Corps competition. The im-

[31] This is particularly true of the CFP. See Henry-René de Bodinat and Michel Chambaud, "L'Influence de l'Etat sur le Secteur Pétrolier Français," *Revue Française de Gestion*, no. 10 (May-June 1977), p. 38.

[32] Dominique Saumon and Louis Puiseux, "Actors and Decisions in French Energy Policy," in *The Energy Syndrome*, ed. Leon N. Lindberg (Lexington, Mass.: Lexington Books, 1978), p. 136.

peratives of adapting to a changing political-economic landscape led the various corps to stake out as much territory as possible, and this has meant certain areas of the economy have become the fiefs of particular corps. Posts in petroleum have generally been conceded to the Corps of Mining Engineers (Corps des Mines). There are, however, notable exceptions that help indicate constraints on the executive's ability to pursue a particular policy. Two particular examples illustrate the problem.

In 1976 Pierre Guillaumat, confronted with obligatory retirement as president of the SNEA, took a distinct interest in the choice of his successor. Generally considered the most influential partisan and defender of the Corps des Mines, Guillaumat's preference was that Corps member and protégé André Giraud, a former director of the DICA, take up duties as Elf's second president. Giscard d'Estaing, preferring someone closer to his own ideological tastes for economic liberalism, eventually nominated former minister Albin Chalandon, a pronounced free market liberal and not incidentally, a member of the Corps of Inspectors of Finance, a competing corps for industrial posts. The ensuing battle over the nomination was fierce and although the President's nominee was eventually installed, the policies that the heretofore liberal Chalandon began to advocate changed dramatically and conformed to the dogma of the company, the defense of industry protectionism. Certainly his new position may have forced a dramatic reevaluation of his long-held beliefs, but it was no secret that the SNEA staff, almost entirely alumni of the Ecole des Mines, was loathe to change routines to conform to the pet philosophies of an *ENArque*, that is, a graduate of the rival Ecole Nationale d'Administration.

It may, of course, be argued that opposition to Chalandon was based on his policy positions rather than his corps membership. In this sense, the battle over the Chalandon nomination resembles that of another Giscard appointment to a high post in the energy sector. The nominee was also ideologically close to Giscard and a member of the Inspection des Finances. When asked if he felt his corps affiliation was a significant factor in the opposition to his candidacy, he was emphatic: "The rivalry between corps was a very significant factor. The fact that I wasn't a member of the Corps des Mines was very important in the opposition to my nomination. But finally it was the fact that I'm a [free market] liberal that brought about the opposition."

It is difficult to gauge from these cases whether the salient opposition was based on policy differences or on corps competition. What is clear is that corps rivalry can be marshalled to the defense of policy interests. Work elsewhere suggests that in fact the process is the reverse, that policy preferences are chosen as a function of their impact on the interests of the corps.[33] This interpretation may be helpful in explaining the appearance of the second French petroleum group, Elf. We noted in Chapter 3 that the creation of a second state firm cannot be explained in simple economic terms. The function fulfilled by Elf—the state-subsidized exploration of North Africa—could have been handled by the CFP. The decision to create a second group has been largely attributed to Pierre Guillaumat. Although Guillaumat was indeed a committed *dirigiste*, he was also a committed partisan of the interests of the Corps des Mines. Establishing a new company rather than directing the CFP to undertake new functions had the effect not only of creating additional jobs, but especially of creating new, high prestige, executive positions. Given also the proclivities of the CFP to promote from within on the basis of long company service,[34] creation of a new firm offered sterling advantages for those interested in finding prestigious positions in an area already conceded to be the province of the Corps des Mines.

The point of the matter here is that policy strategies are

[33] Suleiman, *Elites in French Society*, chap. 7 and *passim*.
[34] De Bodinat and Chambaud, "L'Influence de l'Etat," p. 38.

not developed in a vacuum. Usually debates on policy incorporate considerations of a specific group impact. The literature on interest groups bears long testimony to these considerations, often defining the study of politics in these terms.[35] The study of the impact of bureaucratic interests on policy formulation is much more recent.[36] What is apparently singular about the French case is that the bureaucratic interests cannot be predicted by the organizational function, role, or mission. The Corps des Mines does not necessarily try to influence policy in the direction of greater appropriations for mines, but rather it will tend to espouse policies that increase its importance in any areas of the economy that it has managed to capture or is likely to capture. It is important that the areas that it has captured or sets its sights on are not predictable from its original functional specialization. When all parties in the competition claim to be generalists, capture of new posts becomes a matter of circumstance.

This phenomenon of corps rivalry and its unpredictable impact make coherent policy uncertain. This has recently been borne out in an important study of French nuclear energy strategy.[37] Based on interviews and documentary data, the study concluded not only that corps rivalry can result in conflicting advice to decision makers, but that these conflicts immobilize policy:

> The embarassment of the politician is at its worst when the *nucléocrates* are in disagreement. When the Atomic Energy Commission [province of the Corps des Mines]

[35] See especially the work of Robert Dahl and David Truman. Many other approaches are implicitly if not avowedly pluralist, e.g., the political economy school associated with such authors as Anthony Downs and Mancur Olson.

[36] E.g. Graham Allison, *The Essence of Decision* (Boston: Little, Brown, 1971); John D. Steinbruner, *The Cybernetic Theory of Decisions* (Princeton: Princeton University Press, 1974); the work of James March and Herbert Simon.

[37] Simonnot, *Les Nucléocrates.*

and Electricité de France [province of the Corps des Ponts et Chaussées] are in dispute, the politician is then incapable of deciding the general interest and is constrained to take dilatory measures.[38]

Policy innovation, then, requires one of three circumstances even within the narrow limits of the French policy debate. Either there is agreement among the corps about the new course to follow on the basis of undisputed "technical reasons"; or disagreeing corps are not powerful enough to block policy changes; or conversely, politicians (such as de Gaulle) have at their disposal resources that enable them to inaugurate new policies without the agreement of the corps.

Thus it may be argued that French policy has remained largely unchanged because the current policy reflects the ensconced interests of the Corps des Mines. Attempts to liberalize petroleum policy portend injury to the French companies where the Corps is most influential. Not surprisingly, although adding insult to injury, the Giscard Administration relied upon members of an interloping corps to attempt to implement policy changes. Even though this corps, the Inspection des Finances, is powerful, the best it could produce even with presidential support was a stalemate. Even here new elites have adopted the policies of their predecessors rather than risk a totally recalcitrant organization by leading where no one follows. Moreover, once the Inspection des Finances attained positions in the oil sector, the very policy it was meant to implement became as much a threat to this new corps as it had been to the Corps des Mines.

The assumption here, though, is not that policy is dominated by corps interests in isolation from the dictates of a sector's economic characteristics. Obviously, it would be a flagrant display of economic ignorance were elite interests to be taken as the sole explanation of policy choices.

[38] Ibid., p. 171.

The point, rather, is that policy solutions are not simply the result of "technical" calculation. Arguments that attribute successful policies to a strong state, which is able to impose sacrifices on an unwilling sector in the name of the technically determined national interest, tend to obscure rather than to illuminate the forces at play.[39] Petroleum policy represents the confluence of economic and bureaucratic interests. Certainly, it is in the interest of all the companies now operating in France to maintain the regulatory shelter that has been so profitable in the past. However, the policy inertia is reinforced by the bureaucratic obstacles to change presented by corps interests.

Other Obstacles to Policy Coherence

ENERGY POLICY AND MACROECONOMIC PLANNING

It may be argued that the relatively brief discussion of the role of French planning so far in this study is a glaring lacuna. Certainly studies such as those of Lucas and of Saumon and Puiseux attribute a major role to the Planning Commission, at least in terms of balancing the interests of different sources of energy.[40] The omission here, however, is intentional. The reasons for this deemphasis are essentially two. First, there has been a marked decline in the influence of Commission in recent years and second, it is not clear that French macroeconomic planning has ever really lived up to its favorable press. Recent evidence indicates that much of France's postwar economic success has been erroneously attributed to the value of indicative (i.e., noncoercive) planning, and even Saumon and

---

[39] This theme is recurrent in the work of Peter J. Katzenstein, Stephen D. Krasner, Robert Gilpin, and others. See Bibliography.

[40] N.J.D. Lucas, "The Role of Institutional Relationships in French Energy Policy," *International Relations* 5 (November 1977); Saumon and Puiseux, "Actors and Decisions."

Puiseux are careful to point out the difference between planned energy consumption and economic reality.[41]

The relative lack of Planning Commission influence on petroleum policy was uniformly conceded by all those interviewed during Giscard's tenure of office. An official of the planning office underlined the essential reason: "The Plan has two functions: to provide forecasts and to propose orientations [for different sectors of the economy]. Since orientations for the petroleum sector have been well established for a very long time, it's not particularly bothersome that others tend to minimize the role of the Plan." Thus even in an area where one would expect influence of the Commission, the supposed grand architect of state investment, its role in new petroleum-related investment is minimal. And with regard to company borrowing, an important lever of influence to the extent that the state has very precise powers of selective credit,[42] the Plan has a passive role. It takes oil company borrowing needs into consideration to establish financial perspectives of the French economy. "In this matter," noted the same official, "the Plan plays a forecasting role, but does not make any recommendations as to orientations."

The decline of macroeconomic planning as a significant element in the administration of French economic policy had become conventional wisdom until Mitterrand. Most directly attributed to the ideological proclivities of Giscard d'Estaing, there had, in fact, always been significant opposition to indicative planning. In a sense, the Plan was an attempt to replace conventional politics. As one ob-

[41] For recent evidence, see Mikkal Herberg, "Planning, Politics and Capitalism: National Economic Planning in Britain and France," *Political Studies* 29 (December 1981); Saumon and Puiseux, "Actors and Decisions."

[42] John Zysman has examined this in *Governments, Markets, and Growth: Financial Systems and the Politics of Industrial Change* (Ithaca: Cornell University Press, 1983).

server interviewed for this study put it: "The Plan died before Giscard because since 1960 it [has] tried to be an instrument of social consensus, thus in competition with *le pouvoir politique*. It has served as a critique of the government by showing the gap between the objectives of the Plan and those which were accomplished by the administration."

There are, of course, elements of planning that were particularly inimical to petroleum policy. As opposed to the secretive nature of petroleum operations, the Planning Commission is a process "where everyone has to talk" and where "all the dossiers are on the table."

Government petroleum policy, to the extent that it exists at all, is the product of a small group of discussants. An expert from Parliament, betraying the wistfulness of an outsider, placed the locus of power in "a closed circle of ten or fifteen men, each defending his fief." The participants in that circle have been outlined in the early pages of this chapter, except for some participants whose official capacities may not be related to petroleum.

An example of the latter is Maurice Lauré, president of France's huge nationalized bank, Société Générale. Lauré's contribution also provides an illustration of the circle's penchant for secrecy. Giscard ordered an evaluation of French petroleum policy to be conducted under the direction of Lauré, a close friend of Guillaumat. Ostensibly, the report was a closely guarded secret in order to avoid "speculation in petroleum stocks," yet the findings of the report remained confidential long after it could have had any speculative effect. The report was, however, alleged to contain considerable analysis of the impact of French policy on various social groups: useful information for macroeconomic planning, not to mention political oppositions. Public policy that is both highly elitist and secretive is not amenable to the mechanics of macroeconomic planning.

It should be noted that the arrival of the Mitterrand Administration was largely expected to signal the rebirth of French planning. The appointment of a key political figure as minister of planning, Michel Rocard, and the previous writings of Finance minister Delors all pointed to an important role for planning.[43] Since final interviews for this study were conducted in the early days of the Mitterrand-Mauroy government, the new role for the Plan could only be the subject of speculation. Nevertheless, it should be clear that many of the constraints on effective planning did not disappear with Giscard d'Estaing.

EXTERNAL CONSTRAINTS ON POLICY

The gravest constraint that affects French petroleum policy is the most obvious one: the international nature of petroleum. Indeed, petroleum policy resembles and is, in fact, a part of foreign policy. This is obvious both in terms of the Ministry of Foreign Affair's formal representation on the boards of French oil companies and in the close collaboration of the companies with the Quai d'Orsay. This, of course, says nothing unusual and is hardly specific to France.

More interesting have been the claims that the French petroleum companies have served as instruments of French foreign policy. The record, however, is unclear. Although it would be difficult to substantiate a case of the tail wagging the dog along the lines that radical conspiracy theorists analyze the relationship of the American Majors to U.S. foreign policy,[44] it was apparent from the interviews conducted for this study that French oil companies accede

[43]Jacques Delors, "The Decline of French Planning" and Franco Archibugi, Jacques Delors, and Stuart Holland, "Planning for Development," in *Beyond Capitalist Planning*, ed. Stuart Holland (New York: St. Martin's, 1978).

[44]Although writers in this school vary in their sophistication, the premise usually fits into the marxist instrumentalist approach that views American policies as the products of more or less overt corporate needs. See, for example, Harry Magdoff, *The Age of Imperialism* (New York: Monthly Review Press, 1969).

to the wishes of the foreign ministry only when there is something in it for them.

To take one example as an illustration, the Saudi Arabian deal mentioned in Chapter 3 for about forty million barrels a year (a very substantial proportion of French requirements) was negotiated at the behest of the French government. However, the terms agreed upon were based upon a price of 93 percent of the posted price, that is to say, standard commercial terms.[45] Three years later, the same terms were considered "advantageous" to the companies.[46] It is worth reiterating the remark of a high-ranking Elf executive: "When the state negotiates a contract with an OPEC country, it's because that country wants a higher price [than the going rate]. . . . If the state wants us to negotiate a contract for political reasons, we say, 'You pay for it!' "

The implication of this line of argument is that there is no purpose presently served by French *state-owned* corporations that could not be served by a *privately owned* corporation, even one owned by foreign nationals, provided that the only motives of the corporation are the normal commercial ones. In fact, as noted in Chapter 3 regarding Elf in Algeria, state ownership alone is no guarantee that politically determined policy needs will be served if those needs run counter to commercial considerations.

SIZE, MULTINATIONAL ORGANIZATION, AND PUBLIC
PURPOSES

The fact that oil companies deal with foreign governments does not exhaust the impact of the international environment on French petroleum policy. The market is not only international, it is highly oligopolistic and dominated by multinational firms. Both of these characteristics have affected the ability of the French administration to

[45] *Financial Times* (London), 9 January 1974.
[46] *Les Echos* (Paris), 28 January 1977.

control the impact of petroleum on the French domestic market.

As noted in previous chapters, the minimum size required for a firm to penetrate the world of international petroleum, particularly if the firm is vertically integrated and thus aims to capture new sources of crude, is extremely large. This is one of the reasons for state intervention in the first place. There are two detrimental aspects of large size that affect state control. First, size alone makes the firms difficult to control both because the dictates of rational organization lead to at least some decentralization of authority and, second and more important, because the huge size needed in the petroleum industry lends itself to a multinational form of organization.[47] The multinationalization of state-owned French firms has been encouraged by official policy. The Nora Report urged a more outward orientation for all French firms, and the Ministry of Finance has been particularly well disposed to foreign incorporation because this allows the huge international borrowing activities of the firms to be handled by foreign branches without adverse effect on the French balance of payments. In this sense, there was a more or less conscious trade-off between economic goals and political control.

Although one could argue that the establishment of foreign branches simply represents a convenient legal fiction that masks the true center of decision making,[48] the point can nevertheless be made that establishment in foreign jurisdictions affects policy makers in two ways. First, foreign branches are subject to the constraints of foreign

[47]Chalandon has in fact urged greater decentralization of authority within Elf than was the custom of his predecessor.

[48]This is the official French position on rights of establishment of U.S.-based multinationals in the European Economic Community under Article 54 of the Treaty of Rome. See Harvey B. Feigenbaum, "EC Industrial Policy and Implications for the U.S." Bureau of International Commerce, U.S. Department of Commerce, Washington, D.C., 1972. Mimeograph.

governments. Overall policy that directs the firm, nationalized or not, must take into consideration foreign tax laws, restrictions on capital movements, and the whole panoply of levers by which governments regulate the behavior of corporations installed on their territory. Second and in counterpoint, corporations can use the differences in various national bodies of legislation to minimize the impact of any one government's regulation. This, of course, aside from the "global rationalization of resources,"[49] is the chief attraction of the multinational form of organization. Thus it is not surprising that the CFP, like its private sisters, should minimize the encumbrances of the French authorities by use of tax havens.[50]

If size and activity lead French firms to multinational organization and this in turn allows the firms even greater autonomy in relation to political authorities, it is the configuration of the petroleum market that guides these autonomous firms in directions contradictory to the interest of the domestic economy. It would be going too far to attribute to the petroleum industry all the characteristics of total market control, especially given the rise to prominence of such maverick independents as Italy's ENI or the American independent breakthrough in Libya, but it is not unjustified to describe the organization of the market as an oligopoly.[51] And although the increasing influence of

[49]This is the usual argument in favor of multinationalization. See, e.g., George Ball, "Cosmocorp: The Importance of Being Stateless," in *World Business: Promise and Problems*, ed. Courtney C. Brown (New York: Macmillan, 1970).

[50]This was an allegation of the Schvartz Report.

[51]See especially Paul Frankel, *Mattei, Oil and Power Politics* (New York: Praeger, 1966) for a sympathetic and astute appraisal of the early years of ENI. Recognition of the role of the "independents" has also been given just consideration in Michael Tanzer, *The Political Economy of Oil and the Underdeveloped Countries* (Boston: Beacon Press, 1969); on the situation in Libya see M. A. Adelman, *The World Petroleum Market* (Baltimore: Johns Hopkins University Press, 1972). It is true that the majors now only control 42 percent of the market and the top fifteen firms now control about

producer governments cannot be discounted, as late as 1979 a U.S. government report found petroleum price rises to be the result of market manipulations by the Majors, rather than by OPEC.[52] Indeed, Krasner has argued that the success of OPEC is largely due to the coincidence of its interests with those of the preexisting company cartels.[53]

The point here is that given the clear market orientation imposed on French nationalized firms by the philosophy of the Nora Report, it is to be expected that the CFP and Elf "take their signals from the Majors."[54] The result, then, that France should suffer from the same petroleum inconveniences as countries served only by private firms should hardly come as a shock. The stir that accompanied the Schvartz Report, therefore, was only strange in that the findings were greeted with surprise.

Conclusion: Bargaining, Policy Formulation, and State Autonomy

The extent to which the state can control its appendages is not easy to determine. Certainly the forces at play in the French policy-making apparatus do not ensure economically rational decisions, nor is successful implementation a foregone conclusion once decisions are made. Gauging the extent to which the state can impose itself on the companies is perhaps most difficult because of the

---

60 percent of the market (*World Business Weekly*, 30 June 1980, p. 33). However, the decline in concentration may be deceiving given the advantages of vertically integrated firms. See W. T. Slick, "A View from a Large Oil Company," in *Witness for Oil*, ed. M. E. Canes and P. M. Markun (Washington, D.C.: American Petroleum Institute, 1976), p. 11.

[52] *Wall Street Journal*, 23 November 1979.

[53] Stephen D. Krasner, "Trade in Raw Materials: The Benefits of Capitalist Alliances," in *Testing Theories of Imperialism*, ed. Steven R. Rosen and James R. Kurth (Lexington, Mass.: Lexington Books, 1974), pp. 191ff.

[54] Leon N. Lindberg, "Comparing Energy Policies: Political Constraints and the Energy Syndrome," in *The Energy Syndrome*, ed. Leon N. Lindberg (Lexington, Mass.: Lexington Books; 1978), p. 327.

bargaining process itself. Since much of the debate is informal, the configurations of power and influence between members of the bureaucracy and other participants no doubt change depending upon the issue being decided. In a sense what one finds in this bargaining is a process not unlike Heclo's "issue networks": amorphous pluralistic policy conflicts where principal actors change according to the issue.[55] The difference, however, is that the cast of characters is much more limited in petroleum policy, as are the kinds of issues that come into question.

Petroleum "issue networks" always involve the same ministry and agency representatives and corps interests, but the system is not quite as rigid as American "iron triangles." Flexibility regarding the outcome of debate comes not from the relatively open process of recruitment seen in Heclo's analysis, but rather from the extent to which a particular issue's impact is unclear. Thus, issues such as nominations for bureaucratic posts produce clear battle lines among the corps. But changes on the content of policy, such as the liberalization of price controls on naphtha and fuel oil, may vary depending upon conjunctural elements such as whether introduction of market forces will raise or lower the price, or more adversely affect one company than another. Economic conjuncture will then be a better predictor of the positions of the Treasury, Budget, and technical ministries.

But although the bureaucratic positions on issues may be predictable from economic forecasts, policy outcomes will vary depending on the influence of various individuals. A Pierre Guillaumat may be more likely to hold sway with a General de Gaulle. René Granier de Lilliac, president of the CFP, may be less influential with the policy establishment than his predecessor. As to the problem of accountability or the direction of company policy, some

[55] Hugh Heclo, "Issue Networks and the Executive Establishment," in *The New American Political System*, ed. Anthony King (Washington, D.C.: American Enterprise Institute, 1978).

state auditors may be more committed to the point of view of the company they "control" than others.

However, to reduce the policy process to the simple conflict of personalities or to the pluralistic predictions of group interests is to ignore the extent to which economic and social structure narrow the terms of debate.[56] Not only does the international structure of the market limit the options available to both administrators and executives, but the structure of French society, with its patterns of elite behavior and incentives for *pantouflage*, assure that only certain questions will be asked and only certain points of view will be heard.

The incentive of lucrative and prestigious positions in the private sector limits the autonomy of state elites by implicitly imposing sanctions on those who might offend

[56] It might be helpful at this point to place the findings of this chapter in comparative perspective. An extensive comparative treatment goes beyond the scope of this study. Fortunately, there have already been a number of studies on comparative energy policy. The following excerpt is useful and suggestive: "First, most energy policy systems have been and continue to be dominated by a relatively small, stable and closed circle of organizational elites, and second, energy policy-making is 'incoherent' and 'sectoral,' uncoordinated and reactive, fragmented and 'immobilist'. . . . The technical content of the area [energy] has limited accessibility and has determined the professional origins of the staff and their patterns of recruitment, as well as their relationships with industrial and professional constituencies. Policy makers have been petroleum or coal, or oil or nuclear men. . . . [E]nergy systems are very resistant to change in spite of abundant information that suggests that existing policies are inadequate or counterproductive. . . . The supply orientation combined with a basic faith in technology produce organizational routines that the British chapter characterized as 'selective misperception of uncertainty'. . . . [I]n the absence of action by governmental authorities, energy outcomes may be controlled by the private sector organized along national or international lines by virtue of the influence they have in so many countries over the determination of both energy demand and supply. It is considerations like these that suggest that elite control and public policy fragmentation may be opposite sides of the same coin" (Leon N. Lindberg, "Comparing Energy Policies: Political Constraints and the Energy Syndrome," pp. 333–37).

a prospective employer. This is reinforced and complicated by the incentives of a corps to defend the interests
of a sector it has "colonized." Thus policy making by the
state becomes a reflection of the diverse interests of specific sectors of French society. The state in this sense is both
captured and fragmented.

Economic ideology, propagated by processes of recruitment and socialization, forms a more subtle bond that links
state elites to society. *Dirigisme* and free market liberalism
do not differ on assumptions about how the economic
world operates. Both accept as eternal truths the tenets of
nineteenth-century marginalist theory and the ensuing
views of optimality. This is especially true of the notion
that profit maximization optimizes resource use. Moreover, these assumptions are shared by essentially all of the
builders of West European nationalized industries from
Mitterrand-style socialists to Giscard d'Estaing. They are
the assumptions that produce consistent similarities in
Western European public policies and public enterprises.
We shall examine these similarities in the next chapter.

CHAPTER FIVE

Public Enterprise in Comparative Perspective

> "The time has come," the Walrus said,
> "To talk of many things:
> Of shoes—and ships—and sealing-wax—
> Of cabbages—and kings—
> And why the sea is boiling hot—
> And whether pigs have wings."
>
> Lewis Carroll

The story of public enterprise in Western Europe is one of ambiguous success and misunderstood failure. The argument up to this point has underlined the inadequacies of French petroleum policy and pointed out the perversities of the country's public oil companies. The purpose of the present chapter is to place the case study in context by examining the activities of Elf and the CFP in the light of other public enterprises. If the case were sui generis, its interest would hardly be more than as an anecdote. The value of any case study, of course, is to illuminate generalities.

My argument is that the case of French oil companies is representative rather than anomalous. The tensions between the public interest on the one hand, and profit maximization and managerial autonomy on the other, are repeated not only by other state oil companies, but by public enterprises generally throughout Western Europe. Although many of Europe's public corporations seem to have served state policies in their early years, they have tended to diverge from the path of the public weal as they have become more "successful," that is, larger, more

121

complex, and more profitable. Huge corporations, owned by various European states, make decisions that affect enormous numbers of lives. The doctrines of profit maximization and managerial autonomy have made these firms competing centers of power. When success is determined by the "bottom line," the evidence bespeaks a myopic approach to both politics and economics.

This theme of dysfunctionally independent firms is illustrated in an examination first of the major state-owned oil companies. The comparison is then extended to other public enterprises. Finally, the conclusion of the chapter juxtaposes these findings to our earlier theoretical suppositions about public enterprise developed in Chapter 1.

Oil

State ownership in the oil industry is hardly a rarity. Among the Seven Sisters, British Petroleum (BP) is owned substantially by the British government.[1] Among the independents, the Italian ENI is perhaps the most well known state firm, but there is also considerable state ownership in Germany's VEBA-Deminex.[2] (Included in this list might be the British National Oil Company, but this is not an operating company so much as an intermediary entrusted with responsibility for concessions in the British portion of the North Sea.) Significantly, the 35 percent government-owned Compagnie Française des Pétroles was modeled after BP, and France's public oil company, Elf, imitated Italy's ENI. A glance at the behavior of all of these corporations is enlightening.

To review the argument presented in Chapters 2 and 3, French petroleum firms were given a large measure of in-

---

[1] Until very recently the state share was 51 percent. The Thatcher government has been selling shares to the private sector, aiming at a state-owned residue of 46 percent. *Wall Street Journal*, 7 May 1980.

[2] See M. M. Postan, *An Economic History of Western Europe from 1945 to 1964* (London: Methuen, 1967), chap. 9.

dependence, were encouraged to make a profit, and gave surprised authorities no small displeasure by doing just that, particularly since the firms' performance was at the expense of the French consumer. France has consistently justified its protected and highly lucrative petroleum market in the name of ensuring a sufficient cash flow to the national petroleum companies. These in turn, it was believed, would defend French interests in the international petroleum market. Although offering some balance of payments benefits by finding oil in the franc zone, the companies proved to be very good at collecting money both from the public purse (in subsidies for exploration, etc.) and from French consumers without performing services in exchange that could not be provided by private firms. (French domestic petroleum prices were consistently the highest in Europe.)[3] Not only were the companies capable of collusion, price fixing, and tax "avoidance,"[4] they refused to fulfill contracts negotiated by the Foreign Office on anything other than strict commercial terms. Nor did the French public oil companies provide France with any more security of supply than the international Majors during the oil embargo of 1973–1974, since Elf and the CFP refused to divert deliveries for foreign customers to France.[5]

The case of British Petroleum is similar. BP enjoys a "special relationship" with the British government, which owned 51 percent of the firm until 1980, when the Thatcher government sold off some shares and retained 46 percent of the equity.[6] The government had taken an interest in 1914 to ensure fuel for the Admiralty at reasonable prices.

[3] Farid Saad, "France and Oil: A Contemporary Economic Study," Ph.D. Diss., M.I.T., 1969, p. 175.

[4] Le Monde, 8 November 1974. See also Chapter 3.

[5] Robert B. Stobaugh, "The Oil Companies in the Crisis," Daedalus 104 (Fall 1975), p. 190.

[6] Wall Street Journal, 7 May 1980. The Baldwin government also sold off shares in 1923, but BP was renationalized by the next Labour government. See Anthony Sampson, The Seven Sisters (London: Coronet Books, 1975), p. 73.

At the insistence of Churchill, the Admiralty agreed to let BP (then called Anglo-Persian) act essentially as a private firm, with the exception that the two government representatives on the board of directors could veto actions thought inimical to the government's foreign or military policy. BP's relation to the British government was analogous to the CFP's in France.

The prewar behavior of BP seemed to justify its existence, bringing in oil at prices relatively cheaper than its competitors' and supplying the treasury with a handsome dividend.[7] The company was also intended to be a kind of substitute for British antitrust legislation. (This was also a concern of the French parliament regarding the CFP.) Sampson, noting the influence of American trustbusting, sees the British nationalization as a move "to limit the power of big business. . . . By buying into BP the British government proclaimed that oil was too important to be left to the oil companies."[8]

However, just as in France, the interests of BP as an independent, profit-maximizing firm began to diverge from government policy objectives. Just as the CFP had refused to divert deliveries from foreign customers during the 1973–1974 oil embargo, so did BP. Supplies were cut to Britain despite requests of the Conservative government.[9] The ensuing Labour government had no better luck controlling the corporation. Anthony Wedgewood Benn, then energy minister, complained of a rather cavalier attitude on the part of the 51 percent state-owned company, which had given its administrative overseer only twenty-four hours notice of a deal to take over VEBA's interests in Germany and the same limited notice of its deal with the French regarding the North Sea's Southwest Approaches oil field.[10] The company also made surreptitious pay-

[7] Ibid.
[8] Ibid.
[9] Ibid., p. 276.
[10] *The Times* (London), 18 October 1978.

ments to Italian politicians, undermined the British position on EEC refinery policy, and secretly violated the British economic sanctions against Rhodesia.[11]

The parallels continue. The Italian oil champion, Ente Nazionale d'Idrocarburi (ENI), also has a rather checkered past. Once again one finds a firm whose foundation was based on the idea of service to the state and a case with some success in that regard. Originally created from a collection of fascist-era state enterprises and heir to the natural gas deposits of the Po Valley, ENI is perhaps the case most relevant to France, both because of Italy's similar deprivation of energy resources and because ENI was the model for Elf.

Also conceived of as a trustbuster,[12] the Italian company used low-cost Soviet oil to lower petroleum prices in Italy's domestic market, much to the annoyance of the Majors, while breaking into the international market by offering terms to producer governments considerably more generous than had been the Majors' practice.[13] What is interesting in the case of Italy is that rather than ENI acting as an instrument of state policy, the relationship was in fact the reverse: the state became an instrument of ENI policy.[14] Like CFP and BP, and unlike Elf (in its early stages), ENI financed its expansion out of retained earnings and private sector loans, so the state had very little leverage over the direction taken by ENI.[15] On the other hand, its ambitious president, Enrico Mattei, was able to maneuver the Italian political system adroitly to aid ENI

[11] Ibid. On the last point see also *The New Statesman*, 23 May 1980.

[12] For a duscussion of this aspect of public enterprise, see Paul H. Frankel, *Mattei, Oil and Power Politics* (New York: Praeger, 1966), pp. 157ff.

[13] Michael Tanzer, *The Political Economy of Petroleum and the Underdeveloped Countries* (Boston: Beacon Press, 1969), chap. 4. The Majors were considered to be so upset with Mattei that upon his death in a suspicious plane crash, they felt obliged to declare themselves innocent of wrongdoing.

[14] Frankel, *Mattei, Oil and Power Politics.*

[15] Ibid., p. 167.

goals: Russian oil was negotiated through a state-to-state agreement, taxes on petroleum products were lowered, and the list goes on.[16]

ENI, although showing some of the capacities of a nationalized enterprise to mitigate the effects of oligopoly, also shows the limits of such an enterprise when granted too much independence. The tendency of these firms to develop into political fiefs in France was noted in Chapter 1, but nowhere was the tendency more pronounced than in Italy. ENI became very much the personal vehicle of Mattei. Although this may have been fortunate, given Mattei's populism and disinterest in personal wealth, his policies often owed more to public relations than economic considerations. For example, ENI pursued policies of lower prices by using Soviet oil against the Majors, but this pricing policy was highly selective; it affected gasoline but not industrial fuel oil. This is hardly what one would expect to aid Italian economic growth, where lower-priced industrial energy would have done much to spur and sustain the short-lived Italian "miracle." Cheap fuel also would have improved Italy's international competitive capacity.[17]

There is even some evidence that ENI's "success" as a profitable state enterprise served the long-term interests of the Majors for, in the words of a representative of American oil interests, "if it [ENI] should fall on evil times it would inevitably have to appeal to the government to bail it out and this might be the beginning of a full-fledged [state] monopoly system."[18]

Whatever trustbusting value ENI had seems to have disappeared with Mattei. ENI achieved something of a rapprochement with the Majors after his death, and there

[16]Louis Turner, *Oil Companies in the International System* (London: Allen and Unwin, 1978), p. 61.

[17]Frankel, *Mattei, Oil and Power Politics*, p. 98. Profit margins in the oil industry were, of course, considerable even in pre-OPEC days.

[18]Cited in ibid., p. 110.

is no evidence that the state-owned company provided any greater service to Italy during the 1973–1974 embargo than did its opposite numbers for France or Britain.[19]

Thus the picture seems to vary only slightly from country to country: nationalized oil companies appear at their origins to serve some public interest, either in terms of security of supply (BP), reasonable prices (ENI), or balance of payments (CFP and Elf), but as they grow they develop more and more in common with the international Majors and act accordingly.

But buccaneering public corporations are not limited to the oil sector. Certainly there are peculiarities to the petroleum industry that are not reproduced elsewhere, such as its inherent international characteristics and its long-standing history of anticompetitive behavior, but public firms in other sectors also behave in ways inimical to the broader interests of the home economy.

Multisector State Holding Companies

Perhaps the most inclusive category is the multisector holding company, based on the model of the Italian firm, IRI (Istituto per la Ricostruzione Industriale), which is the most widely imitated public enterprise "success story." Here one finds examples such as Britain's National Enterprise Board, France's Institut pour le Développement Industriel, Sweden's Statsforetag, even Germany's VIAG.[20] All of these have been conscious imitations of the Italian state conglomerate.

IRI is a case where praxis preceded theory. It is a living monument to the collapse of Italian investment banking during the Depression and to Mussolini's subsequent

[19]Turner, *Oil Companies*, pp. 60–61 and 178.

[20]See Stuart Holland, "Adoption and Adaptation of the IRI Formula: Britain, France, Canada, Australia, Sweden, West Germany," in *The State as Entrepreneur*, ed. Stuart Holland (New York: International Arts and Sciences Press, 1972).

bailout of the banks and the major industries they controlled. This haphazard fascist venture into state capitalism has been credited by many as the backbone of democratic Italy's economic miracle of the 1950s and 1960s and has even been applauded as a surrogate for macroeconomic planning by such authorities as Andrew Shonfield.[21] As one might suspect, the record is more problematic.

Although many, especially Holland, hail IRI as an enterpreneur, the company's achievements need to be put into proper context.[22] Indeed, its similarities to British nationalized "failures" (e.g., British Steel) are marked.[23] Scattered over ten sectors in the 1930s, IRI was a predominant influence only in fields where private enterprise was unwilling to risk losses. In fact, companies were often sold back to the private sector as soon as they became profitable.[24] Thus, even in its entrepreneurial role, IRI was essentially a form of complex subsidy to the private sector, absorbing risks while passing on benefits to the rest of the economy. Yet to gauge the impact of managerial autonomy, one needs to assess the effect of IRI's management decisions on more general policy objectives determined by political authorities.

Here it must be noted that Italian legislation, much like that of Great Britain, is meant to promote much more direct political control over IRI activities than is the case, for example, in France. Certainly much of the investment that took place in the underdeveloped South (Mezzogiorno) is the result of IRI investments as broadly directed by Italian law. Yet the obligation to concentrate 60 percent of new

[21] Ibid.; Andrew Shonfield, *Modern Capitalism* (New York: Oxford University Press, 1969), pp. 192ff.

[22] Holland, *The State as Entrepreneur.*

[23] See Richard Pryke, *The Nationalised Industries* (Oxford: Martin Robertson, 1981), chap. 11.

[24] M. V. Posner and S. J. Woolf, *Italian Public Enterprise* (Cambridge: Harvard University Press, 1967), p. 24.

investment in the south is by itself no more constraining than Elf's responsibility to search for oil in the franc zone. In terms of power to allocate resources that affect people's lives, IRI, like the French oil companies, is on a very long tether. Despite more constricting legislation that ties IRI to the Ministry of Public Holdings, the decentralized nature of the Italian political system in fact allows the giant firm to play one political authority off against another.[25] This corporate manipulation of the state, although less publicized than the case of Mattei's ENI, nevertheless marks a consistent thread in Italian, and indeed European, state enterprise.

Prodi has noted that the relationship between IRI and the Ministry of Public Holdings has become the one familiar to students of regulation, where the regulatory authority in fact becomes the industry's representative to the state.[26] As public enterprise comes to resemble private enterprise, its relation to government mirrors that of the private sector:

> The perversion of the relationship between enterprise and government has not been confined to public sector enterprises. While public enterprises have developed a relationship with the Ministry of Public Holdings that might be called "patronage without political purpose," private enterprises have developed the same sort of relationship with the Ministry of Industry.[27]

Certainly Prodi's concept of "patronage without politi-

---

[25] Carol Johnson, "Relations with Government and Parliament" in *The State as Entrepreneur*, ed. Stuart Holland (New York: International Arts and Sciences Press, 1972), pp. 202ff. No equivalent to the centralized Ministry of Public Holdings exists in France or Britain.

[26] See especially Grant McConnell, *Private Power and American Democracy* (New York: Vintage Books, 1966).

[27] Romano Prodi, "Italy," in *Big Business and the State*, ed. Raymond Vernon (Cambridge: Harvard University Press, 1974), p. 61.

cal purpose" narrowly defines what is political, because the implications of this relationship for public policy become clearer in the ensuing discussion:

> A second parallel has been evident between the behavior of the Ministry of Industry and that of the Ministry of Public Holdings. Traditionally, the research office of Confindustria [the Italian national employers' association] has played the role of ghost writer to the Ministry of Industry, while the same kind of relationship has existed between public industry and the Ministry of Public Holdings.[28]

It is one thing to establish that Italian state enterprise benefits from a considerable degree of managerial autonomy vis-à-vis political authorities. It is quite another to show a link between such autonomy and corporate actions that conflict with public goals. As with the cases we have noted thus far, such conflicts appear in the case of IRI.

Even in the area of employment in the Mezzogiorno, where IRI has been most consistently applauded, many have noted that in this region of underutilized labor, investment has been strangely capital intensive.[29] Although Prodi attributes capital intensive investment to unnamed "political forces" who prefer the simpler incentive technique of allocating capital rather than labor, this does not explain why a technique that supposedly permits more precise targeting of investment was so suboptimally used.[30] For example, selective capital allocations were not used to create a set of firms in the south that could use each other's products. This would have allowed firms to reduce current costs such as transport while providing the basis for sustained development. Instead, IRI created isolated

[28] Ibid., p. 62.
[29] Posner and Woolf, *Italian Public Enterprise*, p. 116.
[30] Prodi, "Italy," p. 61.

investment "oases" in the Mezzogiorno's economic desert.[31]

The answer to this misallocation of capital and ill-served public purpose may lie in both the profit-maximizing behavior and the conglomerate nature of IRI. Given IRI's strong position in various capital-goods producing industries, the huge firm's investment decisions can be understood as creating profitable sales opportunities for different (and relatively unrelated) capital goods producers within the IRI system.[32] In the Italian context, this becomes reverse cross-subsidization in the sense that funds earmarked for investment in the south actually benefit IRI suppliers in the north, while the south in turn bears the opportunity cost of suboptimal investment.

IRI's method of financing has also been detrimental to overall public policy. Supposedly as a way to inject market discipline, IRI issues debt on domestic capital markets with no unified supervision. Because of IRI's size, this weakens the Italian Treasury's control of capital and money markets. It is interesting that one finds no dearth of Italian theorists (especially Saraceno and Prodi) who justify public enterprise in terms of the inapplicability of countercyclical macroeconomic techniques.[33] In fact, with the state's fiscal and monetary leverage so weakened, these Keynesian solutions may be inapplicable *because* of these independent public enterprises.

Much of IRI's financing, as Holland notes with guarded approval, is also raised by sale of the equity (often up to 49 percent) of its subsidiaries.[34] This presents a problem, as Posner and Woolf point out:

[31] Cf. Posner and Woolf, *Italian Public Enterprise*, p. 111.

[32] I am grateful to James R. Kurth for suggesting this to me.

[33] Saraceno is cited in Stuart Holland, "State Entrepreneurship and State Intervention," in *The State as Entrepreneur*, ed. Stuart Holland (New York: International Arts and Sciences Press, 1972), p. 6.

[34] Stuart Holland, "The Finance Formula," in *The State as Entrepreneur*, ed. Stuart Holland (New York: International Arts and Sciences Press, 1972), pp. 196–99.

Although selling equities is an attractive way of raising money, it only works if the equities are in fact the direct obligations of a firm or a holding company which is known to be profitable. In practice, this means that state enterprises which raise money by the sale of equities are passing on parts of their profits to the private sector. Such profits could better be employed in reducing the gearing ratio of other firms in the public sector whose prospects are not so favorably regarded by a market naturally inclined to weigh evident profitability above longer-term considerations.[35]

Assuming that public firms are created for reasons other than simply maintaining their own existence, once again it appears that allowing state firms the autonomy to pursue profit maximization leads to operations that conflict with long-term public goals. Indeed, the lack of independence of Italian firms from money and capital markets makes them dependent upon the growth of the economy for their own investment resources. Rather than promote growth, it appears that IRI is in fact as passive as the British nationalized "failures" such as British Steel and the Electricity Board.[36] IRI's very independence from finance controlled by political authorities reduces its capacity as an instrument of growth. Thus IRI weakens Keynesian tools of demand management while, presumably, absorbing private investment that might have fired other sectors.[37]

Banks

The relationship of national enterprise and finance requires some examination of the role of nationalized banks.

[35] Posner and Woolf, *Italian Public Enterprise*, p. 117.

[36] Compare ibid. and Stuart Holland, *The Socialist Challenge*, (London: Quartet Books, 1975), pp. 146ff and *passim*.

[37] This, of course, is similar to the monetarist problem of "crowding out."

In many ways banks may replace holding companies as a form of multisector nationalization. In Austria, one finds not only the Österreichische Industrierverwaltung-Aktiengesellschaft (OIAG), an alpine equivalent to IRI, but a good deal of Austrian industry enters the public sector by virtue of equity acquired by nationalized banks. Sixty thousand Austrians are employed by companies so owned, and together with over 100,000 employed by OIAG, account for about one-fifth of the country's industrial production.[38]

Much like IRI, preservation of employment has been an ostensible aim of the public banking sector, which has bailed out many failing enterprises in the private sector and cross-subsidized public firms in similar positions, especially in the steel industry.[39] As in Italy, Austrian public enterprise has not so much served policy as created it. For a good deal of Austria's postwar history this was made possible by the apparent domination of supervisory boards by the political parties in proportion to their electoral strength, that is, by the *Proporz*. Shonfield has remarked that this device, which gave the appearance of political control of the board of directors, "had the result of downgrading parliament."[40] Control of the economy for all practical purposes was left to "technocratic" managers with the result that "the managers of the undertakings run things pretty much their own way so long as they make sure to respond demonstratively every now and then to the distant bark of the parliamentary watchdog tethered to his post."[41]

The price demanded for Austrian state bank assistance has consistently been extreme labor discipline, that is, enforcement of low wages, which has limited wage concessions to among the lowest of the advanced industrial

[38]"Austria Survey," *The Economist*, 15 March 1980, p. 10.
[39]Ibid., p. 10.
[40]Shonfield, *Modern Capitalism*, p. 193.
[41]Ibid., p. 195.

countries.[42] Indeed, although the usual arguments for the success of Austria's "incomes policy" attribute the major role to the country's neocorporatist form of interest organization,[43] a case could well be made that the chief instrument of wage repression is the nationalized banks. These offer financial bailouts to industries in exchange for limiting wage demands. In this sense the Austrian nationalized banks play a role analogous to that of the International Monetary Fund toward supplicant countries in balance of payments trouble. The solution in both cases is classically deflationary.

The impact of nationalized banks in France has, perhaps, been more nefarious. Just as IRI has been criticized as a "state within a state," although not to the point, as in Austria, of having replaced the state, public banking and public interest have hardly been synonymous concepts in France. Stoffaës and Victorri point out that the central bank was nationalized progressively in 1936 and 1945 precisely because of continual opposition to the policies of center-left governments.[44] It was assumed (wrongly) that nationalization of France's largest banks would also permit greater public control of economic policy.

The pattern of bank nationalizations in France was consistent with nationalization is other sectors. The state claimed ownership but was content to avoid any real control, except in the nomination of the banks' directors. The parallel with the French oil industry is in fact very close. For just as the state has promoted a cartel in the oil industry by apportioning and protecting the domestic market—partially to ensure the solvency of the public oil firms—so too did it pursue a similar policy for the nationalized banks. Stoffaës and Victorri, rarely critical of official

---

[42] "Austria Survey," *The Economist*, 15 March 1980, p. 10.

[43] E.g., Gerhard Lehmbruch, "European Neo-Corporatism: An Export Article?," Woodrow Wilson Center, Washington, D.C., 26 April 1982.

[44] Christian Stoffaës and Jacques Victorri, *Nationalisations* (Paris: Flamarion, 1977), p. 97.

policies, note that "a veritable cartel was organized by the profession [i.e., the banking sector] and was supported by the government; the latter would perhaps have been more severe had it not been concerned with constantly assuring the profitability of the nationalized firms."[45] Just as in the case of oil, French nationalized banks, including the world's largest bank (by deposits), the Banque Nationale de Paris, could hardly be identified as more public-spirited than their brethren. These banks have pursued inflationary interest and money creation policies,[46] diverted investment out of France, and then speculated against the franc.[47] Moreover, the nationalized banks were more recalcitrant than private banks in applying the government's credit directives of 1973–1975.[48]

Once again, the literature on public enterprise finds use for the appellation "a state within a state," this time applying it to nationalized banks in France.[49] In the words of one observer, "monetary developments since nationalization leave the impression that these banks have behaved more like barons than agents of the state."[50]

Managerial Autonomy, Profitability, and "Success"

This review has emphasized that the goal of profitability and the accordance of managerial autonomy to pursue that goal may result in the subversion of broader public policies, even in sectors that are apparently competitive. Moreover, even where public enterprise has been successful according to microeconomic criteria, the success often

[45] Ibid., p. 109.
[46] Philippe Simonnot, *Le Pouvoir Monétaire* (Paris: Seghers, 1975), p. 166. Banks that do not structure their principal loans in long-term fixed interest contracts are not handicapped by inflation as is popularly assumed. I am grateful to Nathaniel Beck for pointing this out.
[47] Stoffaës and Victorri, *Les Nationalisations*, p. 110.
[48] Ibid.
[49] Simonnot, *Le Pouvoir Monétaire*, p. 166.
[50] Ibid., pp. 166–67.

has more to do with a favorable macroeconomic environment (i.e., economic growth or industrial decline) than with individual management decisions or the organization of particular state firms. For it is the economic environment that structures both the demand for the products of the public sector (e.g., electricity, steel) and many of its costs. In this sense, the failure of an enterprise may have less to do with its management criteria than with the determining characteristics of the industry's place in the economy. Even Pryke, who is largely critical of nationalized industries' performance, notes that:

> It would be wrong to attribute the nationalized industries' failings simply to public ownership. Almost any collection of British industries would have shown up badly. . . . Moreover the operation of industries that belong to the public enterprise sector poses particular problems because they tend to be natural monopolies and/or be in decline. Many of the weaknesses which appear from the British experience to be a consequence of public ownership are displayed in the same industries abroad under private ownership.[51]

Economies in crisis provoke challenges to prevailing orthodoxies. Compare the following quotations:

> The idea that socialization and public control necessarily mean administration directly by the Government department dies hard, but is dying in every country. The importance of flexibility and expert management on the one hand and freedom from party domination on the other hand, has so far been recognized that . . . the tendency is to secure public control and elimination of the profit motive while keeping the actual management in the hands of a body not susceptible to party political pressure and interference.[52]

[51] Pryke, *The Nationalised Industries,* p. 265.
[52] Herbert Morrison, *Public Control and Regulation of Industry and Trade*

The issues of public policy involved are so large and politically sensitive that it is not realistic to suppose that they would ever be left for long to the management [of public firms] alone to determine, subject only to periodic checks on their financial performance.[53]

The first was written by Herbert Morrison, minister of transport in the first Labour government of 1929. The second emanated from the British National Economic Development Office in 1979. Both are meant as critiques of prevailing orthodoxies, Morrison targeting the state socialism of the Left, the NEDO Report targeting the state capitalism of the technocratic Right.

The question then becomes, why do prevailing orthodoxies prevail? It is the Morrisonian orthodoxy that holds sway in the advanced industrial societies of the West. It is defended by social democrats of the Left and technocrats of the Right. I would argue that this is not accidental, for it permits public enterprise to be compatible with fundamentally capitalist economies, economies which fall occasionally under the stewardship of governments that are nominally socialist or overtly conservative. If the profit motive were to be rejected in one sector of the economy (where a public firm might be operating), it would be a short step to apply this logic to other sectors where public firms did not yet exist. In this sense the doctrines of managerial autonomy and profit maximization act as limits on the power of the state.

How do we then reconcile this with the discussion of state power at the beginning of this study? A reconciliation requires once again the theoretical separation of the two concepts that are usually taken together: *power* and

---

(1932) quoted in Martyn Sloman, *Socializing Public Ownership* (London: Macmillan, 1978), p. 7.

[53]NEDO report, quoted in M. R. Garner, "The White Paper on Nationalised Industries: Some Criticisms," *Public Administration* 5 (Spring 1979), p. 8.

autonomy.[54] States may be powerful in that they can impose specific policy solutions like nationalization on certain elements of their societies, while nevertheless acting in the interest (if not under the direction)[55] of other elements in a society. States may serve specific interests in the name of the general interest. If one considers nationalizations that are essentially bailouts or private sector subsidies another typology, shown in Table 5.1, is suggested.

To the extent that nationalization of lame ducks represents the transfer of losses from private owners to the entire polity, public enterprise indicates the capture of state policy by private interests. To the extent that the state resells the enterprises after returning them to profitability (as the Thatcher and Mussolini governments did), the relationship remains one of private sector domination.

Conclusion

The question of political control of public corporations has been answered uniformly throughout Western Europe. Governments have for the most part publicly forsworn interference in the operation of nationalized industry. This is as true of the socialist government of François Mitterrand as of the conservative government of Valéry Giscard d'Estaing. It is as true of the Morrisonian corporation of Britain as the "enterpreneurial" holdings of Italy. Public firms in "competitive" sectors are told to maximize profits and are accorded the independence to do so.

Although the inapplicability of profit criteria in "natural monopoly" sectors such as public utilities has been long recognized, increased concentration in almost all industrial sectors has made assumptions about competition, which is the foundation of neoclassical economics, highly

---

[54]Consider here the treatment of state power popular among the neo-mercantilist school of political economists, e.g., see Chapter 1, note 39.

[55]This is obviously difficult to document.

TABLE 5.1. Public Policy and the Autonomy of the State

	Policy	Example	Diffusion of Losses	
Increasing concentration of losses	Laissez faire	No bailouts	Concentrated	*Increasing state autonomy*
	Incentive-disincentive schemes	State loan guarantees	More diffuse	
	Regulation	Public utilities (U.S.)	Consumers bear costs	
	Nationalization	Steel industry (U.K. and France)	Most diffuse	

questionable. Profitability may indicate efficient production in a competitive market, but the tendency is for nationalized industry to share in monopoly rents with their private sector brethren, where cartels are possible. This is not only true of French banks and oil companies, where anticompetitive behavior has historically been obvious. Neoclassical principles have long been askew in such nominally competitive sectors as automobiles: neither Renault nor General Motors felt compelled to lower prices despite a precipitous fall in demand after the oil crises of 1974 and 1979. Why should firms organized exactly as those in the private sector, responding independently to the incentives of highly imperfect markets, act any differently than those that are privately owned? If it is indeed the incentive structure of highly concentrated markets that has led to modern economic difficulties such as prices rising with a ratchet-effect and decreasing productivity, nationalization à l'Européenne offers no solution.

The failures and "successes" of public enterprise should encourage us to look more closely at a body of theory that is becoming increasingly irrelevant to the modern world economy. Microeconomics, deriving from a time when markets were clearly competitive and preaching the social benefits of individual profit maximizers, solves few problems in a world that no longer resembles the theory's ideal. However, some of the solutions of the Left may be no better. Workers' control of factories, for instance, in no way limits the conflict between producers and consumers: "No one in the Labour Movement would argue," one observer notes, "that the hospitals should be run for the benefit of the doctors."[56]

Desperation leads to change, or so one would assume. The combined phenomena of unemployment and inflation that have characterized the economies of the West in the 1970s and 1980s heralded major government changes, with the *vox populi* apparently endorsing dramatic economic experiments.

The availability of public enterprise as an instrument of national economic policy clearly distinguishes some nations from others and may indeed reflect the power of particular states, or in Samuel Huntington's apt phrase, their "degree of government."[57] Yet in political economy, differences in *degree* may not be as important as differences in *kind*. In whose interest does a powerful state operate? Who makes the sacrifices, who pays the cost? Simply assuming a state's activities to be in the public interest has long been considered dangerous. Similar assumptions about the flowering of public enterprise may bear poisonous fruit.

[56] Sloman, *Socializing Public Ownership*, p. 117.
[57] Samuel P. Huntington, *Political Order in Changing Societies* (New Haven: Yale University Press, 1968), p. 1.

CHAPTER SIX

Conclusion: Où Est l'Etat?

> [If you accept a doctrine and allow it] to go
> on and grow, you will awaken some day to
> find it standing over you, the arbiter of your
> destiny, against which you are powerless,
> as men are powerless against delusions.
>
> William Graham Sumner

> For twenty years after the War, I used to say
> our situation was like the man falling from
> a skyscraper. As he passed the fourteenth
> floor he called out, "It's not too bad so far."
>
> Joan Robinson

When the findings of the Schvartz Report were made public
in 1974, the question that dominated the headlines was "Où
est l'état?" (Where is the state?). Perhaps a more fitting
question might be, "What is the state?" More specifically,
one might ask if nationalized firms form a part of the state.
In that they have behaved in ways that contradict the
broader policy aims of political authorities, can one conceive of a state at war with itself? Can one reconcile this
behavior with the way social scientists and philosophers
have viewed the state in the past?

These are the questions that have guided and informed
the present study. Naturally, our observations of political
reality are shaped largely by our choice of what to ob-
serve; thus it is noted from the outset that findings bear
the imprint of the observer's sociological tastes. Nevertheless, the advantage of a case study is that it examines con-
crete events that in some way affect people's lives.

The implications of this case study are perhaps even more
dramatic in light of the major changes that took place in

141

French politics after the elections of May and June 1981 when, for the first time in twenty-three years, a left-of-center government occupied the Elysée and Palais Bourbon. This is especially interesting since the Socialist government made nationalization the centerpiece of its economic policy and extended the French public sector to a magnitude unmatched by any western industrialized country.

The organization of the public sector under Mitterrand remained remarkably similar to the organization under his predecessors, and that alone has important political implications. But that gets ahead of the purpose of this chapter, which is to discuss the implications of this case study of French petroleum policy, first by examining possible alternative strategies and second, by trying to explain why those strategies were not adopted. Through the latter, a broader view of the case's significance can be established.

The Alternatives: The Paths Not Taken

THE REGRESSIVE IMPACT OF FRENCH PETROLEUM POLICY

We noted in Chapters 2 and 3 that French petroleum policy has resulted in a high cost to the French economy with marginal social benefits. Under the guise of ensuring security of supply, France has consistently implemented an expensive policy of protectionism. French consumers of petroleum products have paid high prices to maintain a French industry which in turn has not acted demonstrably different from non-French firms. Since the high cost of petroleum products also drives up the equilibrium price of substitute energy sources, French oil protectionism has raised the price of all goods that require energy—that is to say, everything—and the effect has been very much like a regressive sales tax.[1] This can be viewed as all the more

---

[1] The extent to which the increased costs can be passed on to the con-

CONCLUSION

regressive when one considers the portion of state revenues obtained from taxes on petroleum products (see Table 2.1). As these taxes have replaced more progressive
forms of taxation, French petroleum policy has been dou-
bly regressive.[2]

However, this kind of criticism is not meaningful unless
one considers the options available to French decision
makers. By examining those options, one gains a clear idea
of the broader constraints on the French state. It is only
then that we can begin to analyze the relationship of state
to society.

THE OPTION OF *Liberalisme*

At the time of most of this study's interviews, the principal debate in France over petroleum policy involved the
extent to which the prices for petroleum should be determined by the "free" market. The latter was favored by
Giscard and the *"libéraux"* (that is, those who favored a
less interventionist policy). Government perception of the
oil market as competitive was crucial. However, although
the old days of a solidly enforced private petroleum cartel

---

sumer is a function of the market position of each industrial user. As
one study indicated, "Certain enterprises which have a poor market position cannot pass along their cost increases, while others favor an inflationary atmosphere to maintain or increase their profits" (C. Gabet, G.
Honoré, and F. Houssin, "Les Répercussion Mécaniques des Hausses des
Prix Energétiques," *Economie et Statistique* no. 56 [May 1974], p. 42).

[2] A gasoline tax is even more regressive when it is considered that lower-
income groups tend to drive older and less fuel-efficient automobiles, although this is mitigated in cities where public transportation is a realistic
alternative. See James P. Stucker, "The Distribution Implications of a Tax
on Gasoline," *Policy Analysis* 3 (Spring 1977), p. 179 and *passim*. For a
comparative study of gasoline taxation, see Alan A. Tait and David R.
Morgan, "Energy and the Role of Gasoline Taxation," *Finance and Development* 17 (June 1980). It is interesting in this regard that the Mitterrand-
Mauroy government reduced the corporate tax rates while raising the more
regressive value-added tax. *Le Monde,* 19 April 1982.

143

are gone,[3] the international oil market has still been far from the ideal type of atomized price-takers envisioned by Adam Smith and his neoclassical descendants. Despite the newer entrants into the world of oil, the market is still highly concentrated and oligopolistic.[4]

A "liberal" policy would not change the structure of the international market. *Dirigisme* has protected the French national champions, but by mandating the firms to operate commercially and maximize profits, the state has only added two more participants to the market. The dynamics of oligopoly have remained substantially unchanged.

Price Effects. A domestic market that left the smaller French oil companies unprotected would certainly result in marginally lower prices in the short run—if the Majors actually competed with each other on the basis of price. This kind of competition is not obvious, but the tenacity with which both the Majors and the two French firms have fought to retain the Law of 1928 suggests there might be some downward pressure on prices if the legislation were repealed, particularly if high prices do not reflect scarcity of crude petroleum.

In this vein, the pseudoliberation of petroleum prices that took place under the Socialists is enlightening.[5] The new system allowed prices to be set "automatically" according

---

[3] The Majors now control only about 42 percent of the market. I am grateful to Peter F. Cowhey for emphasizing this point to me.

[4] The top fifteen firms now control about 60 percent of the market (*World Business Weekly*, 30 June 1980, p. 33). This figure is somewhat low for traditional measures of oligopoly, but both price/cost figures and the relatively high cost of establishing an *integrated* firm still suggest that the market is oligopolized. For the advantages of vertically integrated oil companies, see W. T. Slick, "A View from a Large Oil Company," in *Witness for Oil*, ed. M. E. Canes and P. M. Markun (Washington, D.C.: American Petroleum Institute, 1976), p. 11; see also J. Huré, "La Politique Française du Pétrole, I," *Revue des Deux Mondes*, 16 April 1966, p. 554.

[5] *Le Monde*, 17 April 1982.

to a complex formula that linked prices partially to the world market price, partially to the Rotterdam spot market price, and partially to an average of prices in six EEC countries. The actual effect was to set a floor on French domestic oil prices while giving the appearance that these prices were set apolitically, since specific actions by public officials would no longer be necessary to maintain company profit margins.[6]

Although the effects of the post-1981 oil glut make the point obvious, other evidence also suggests that overall price levels would be lower if France were to abandon protectionism. For instance, since Elf has been more heavily involved in the supply of industrial fuels for the production of electricity, protective policies in this product line would be expected to have particularly far-reaching effects. If French energy costs have indeed been higher than those of free market competitors, this might partially explain Germany's greater ease in paying its import bill with the earnings of its more competitive exports.[7] Lower oil prices would also have made France's ambitious nuclear energy program considerably less attractive, because it is a program that effectively locks France into high energy costs.[8]

Balance of Payments Effects. These impacts on international competitive capacity are particularly important in considering the most substantial defense of French petroleum policy. There can be no doubt of the positive balance of payments effects that were the result of Elf's exploration in the franc zone. A free market option would certainly not have led to an early exploration of the Sa-

[6] Ibid. Why the Socialists did this will be discussed below.

[7] Horst Mendershausen, *Coping with the Oil Crisis* (Baltimore: Johns Hopkins University Press, 1976), pp. 67ff.

[8] Stephen S. Cohen, "Informed Bewilderment," in *France in the Troubled World Economy*, ed. Stephen S. Cohen and Peter A. Gourevitch (London: Butterworth, 1982), p. 39.

hara. However, the domestic prices required to pay for the search may in the long run have had a deleterious effect on the balance of payments by doing injury to the overall competitive capacity of French industry. Above-average energy costs would certainly increase the prices of French exports or, more nefariously, would provide an incentive for the imposition of wage restraints on France's poorly organized work force. This is particularly true since productivity gains via greater general capital intensity have in the past meant the introduction of energy intensive technology.

Security of Supply Effects. The free market solution seeks security of supply through the Majors' own attempts to diversify their sources of crude. The assumption of French policy is that the foreign-owned Majors are less reliable than French companies but this, as noted in Chapter 3, has not been borne out by events. When the Majors diverted oil during the 1973–1974 crisis, the French firms were of no great assistance in compensating for the loss to the domestic market.

The French have sought security of supply via state-to-state contracts and barter agreements. Yet state firms have been reluctant to act as instruments for these agreements on other than commercial terms. Since the state-to-state deals were highly profitable, a similar function could have been fulfilled by private, non-French companies. Here, the policy of support to national champions chosen by French authorities differs little from the results of the free market solution.

Thus, a free market solution similar to the path taken by Germany, for example, would not be very different from French *dirigisme* in terms of actual impact, with the exception that in specific areas the French solution has been even costlier to its inhabitants than reliance on the international Majors.

CONCLUSION

THE OPTION OF REORGANIZING THE PUBLIC SECTOR

It has been a theme of this study that the profit-maximizing orientation of French public enterprise, combined with managerial autonomy, leads to behavior that is inconsistent with the purported goals of French petroleum policy. How would the elimination of this structure and a change in incentives affect achievements of the French state in the petroleum sector?

Part of the problem with the current structure of French public enterprise is its incentive to keep the state as much in the dark as possible about its costs. This was shown in the Schvartz Report's ·discovery of pricing irregularities, where public firms had an interest in overestimating their costs so that domestic prices would be set even higher than simple protectionism would dictate. My assumption is that companies relieved of an incentive to maximize profits would also be relieved of at least one incentive to obscure costs. This would lead to a proliferation of advantages for public policy in the oil industry.

Public Firms as Yardsticks. At the least controversial level, one can justify use of public enterprise as a yardstick by which to measure the performance of private firms under conditions of imperfect competition. This justification has a venerable tradition in the defense of nationalization, but yardsticks with measures falsely drawn are of little use. Incentives for distortion need to be removed.

The example of the Tennessee Valley Authority is illuminating. Operating as a publicly owned utility with a return on investment, but not a mandate to *maximize* that return, TVA not only fueled industrialization in the South, but provided downward pressure generally on energy prices in the United States.[9] In addition, the use of com-

---

[9]Stefan H. Robock, "An Unfinished Task: A Socio-Economic Evaluation of the TVA Experiment," in *The Economic Impact of TVA,* ed. John R. Moore (Knoxville: University of Tennessee Press, 1967), p. 107.

147

petitive bidding by the utility focused attention on price fixing by subcontractors, indicating that profit maximization is not a necessary incentive to lower costs.[10]

In the French context of administered oil prices, a trustworthy window on costs in the petroleum industry, accurately showing what companies actually paid out, would have reduced the inflationary pressures inherent in present practice. An administration that is dependent upon the good will of corporations, even those headed by the "great public servants," the *grands commis de l'état*, is necessarily at a disadvantage. As French public firms have been essentially autonomous in order to pursue profits unfettered, the state has been dependent upon the public-spiritedness of enterprise directors. Yet different executives have different conceptions of the public interest, and almost any action can be justified in the long-term interest of the state. To reiterate an earlier illustration, even in the uniformly conservative administration of Giscard d'Estaing, managers and ministers tended to be at cross purposes. As we noted in Chapter 3, Industry minister Giraud and Elf president Chalandon were at loggerheads over the disposition of Elf's profits, especially the attempts to use them to purchase Kerr-Magee and then Texasgulf. Even considering the conflict of personalities, the dispute could have been explained in terms of legitimate differences of opinion. Chalandon aimed Elf's cash flow at the purchase of foreign energy and mining companies; Giraud wanted the profits plowed into new exploration. Chalandon could justify his strategy in terms of the advantages of size and diversity in international competition; Giraud could justify his choice in terms of directly satisfying France's future energy needs.[11] (Ultimately, and ironically, Chalandon won by convincing the Socialists that allowing him to

[10] Ronald H. Wolf, "Identical Pricing and TVA: Toward More Effective Competition," in *The Economic Impact of TVA*, ed. John R. Moore (Knoxville: University of Tennessee Press, 1967).

[11] See *Le Monde*, 1 August 1980.

pursue his strategy would reassure the business community, by showing that French nationalizations were to be run as "serious," apolitical businesses.)[12]

Since public enterprise managers, expected to emphasize the importance of the bottom line, may have a variety of reasons for disagreeing with the government, one might remove some of this friction by changing the implicit notions of what constitutes success. Eliminating the incentives to obscure the firm's costs (i.e., the incentive to cheat) could make executives' or firms' good will more certain. If profit maximization were not the bottom line, their cooperation might be more readily assumed.

Information and Planning. The Socialists' accession to power in 1981 was accompanied by popular expectation and verbal assurance that French macroeconomic planning was going to have a new place in the sun. But after a year in office and despite the considerable political influence of Planning minister Michel Rocard, the Plan was still in the winter of its discontent. Although macroeconomic planning had been anathema to the neoliberalism of Giscard d'Estaing, its place in the industrial policy of his successors hardly extended beyond rhetorical genuflection.[13] Managerial autonomy and macroeconomic planning are concepts that are at best conflictual, if not contradictory. Accepting the former reduces the effectiveness of the latter. They may not, however, be mutually exclusive, if planning is "indicative," that is, noncoercive.

To the extent that French indicative planning has found

[12] *New York Times,* 14 November 1981.

[13] Giscard opposed the Plan for ideological reasons, and many French businessmen and bureaucrats alike have always been reluctant to *"mettre les dossiers sur la table."* As one of Giscard's advisors informed me, "The Plan has always been an implicit criticism of *les pouvoirs publics,* a reminder of what politicians have not accomplished." For a study of the politics of planning, see Stephen S. Cohen, *Modern Capitalist Planning: The French Model* (Berkeley and Los Angeles: University of California Press, 1977). See also Chapter 4 above.

its justification as an exchange of information,[14] public firms which have an incentive to provide accurate information about key sectors could provide yeoman's service. Since this information reduces uncertainty and therefore guards against the creation of various forms of excess capacity, one might expect to achieve macroeconomic benefits in efficiency if public enterprises were reoriented. This is quite the reverse argument of the Nora Report which, by focusing on the microeconomic level, argues for a profit orientation to improve the efficiency of the firm. Clearly, a more systemic approach to economic problems would have avoided this "misapplication of microeconomic theory."[15]

"Reindustrialization." This leads us to a closer examination of how reorienting the incentives of France's national champions might assist in the rejuvenation of French industry. Since the state is responsible for the functioning of the economy as a whole, too close an attention to the micro-level may blind authorities to certain advantages of a broader approach. It is a matter of conventional wisdom that students of management are taught to avoid organizing enterprises as collections of individual profit centers, because this form of organization—as opposed to cost centers—disguises possibilities for economies of scale. Reinforcing the profit orientation of public enterprise in basic sectors precludes the possibility of, say, using such firms to subsidize industries and exports through a cheap fuels policy. By protecting the profitability of French oil companies through high domestic prices, present policy has meant that the French economy has been subsidizing the oil industry. To the extent that the French "jam pot" has

[14]Jean-Claude Casanova, *Principes d'Analyse Economique* (Paris: Les Cours de Droit, 1968–1969), p. 646.

[15]Alec Nove, *Efficiency Criteria for Nationalised Industries* (Toronto: University of Toronto Press, 1973). See also his "Recent Developments in Eastern European Economics," in *Post Industrial Society,* ed. Bo Gustafsson (London: Croom Helm, 1979), p. 138.

allowed greater profits to the Majors, which reinvest their profits outside of France, French policy has accentuated the problems of capital hemorrhage.[16] This has been aggravated by the tendency of the national firms to mimic their big sisters in the rush to invest in companies abroad instead of exploring for oil.[17]

Disincentives to Cartelization. It might justifiably be argued that the possible gains of a non-profit-maximizing petroleum corporation are limited by the nature of the market in which such a firm would operate.[18] Certainly, it is possible to suppose that the small size of even a combined Elf-CFP and the nature of OPEC price setting would severely limit the possible gains of a reorganized public oil corporation. Why worry about the price of a drop in the bucket?

Here one might pose two arguments. First, it is not at all clear that OPEC's power as a price maker in the world market is either real or, if real, durable. When one very highly placed executive in Elf was interviewed in 1979, he declared that "Only Kuwait has taken charge of its own production."

Second, the percentage of world production accounted for by OPEC is likely to decrease significantly over the next few years.[19] What is clear is that none of the present petroleum corporations, the French companies included, have

[16]M. A. Adelman, "The Multinational Corporation in World Petroleum," in *The International Corporation*, ed. Charles P. Kindleberger (Cambridge: M.I.T. Press, 1970), p. 238.

[17]French authorities are not blind to this problem. Some officials interviewed talked at length of the problems of ensuring that Elf's foreign investment would result in employment effects in France. Indeed, recent cleavages in the administration involved exploration versus foreign diversification (*Le Monde*, 18 July and 1 August 1980). See above pp. 83–84.

[18]To say a firm would not maximize profit does not preclude a fixed return on capital. See below.

[19]Arnold Safer, *International Oil Policy* (Lexington, Mass.: Lexington Books, 1979), pp. 15ff.

151

any incentive not to collaborate with the cartel in the maintenance of artificially high prices.

This is not to say, however, that were the French companies relieved of the need to maximize profits they would necessarily be able to produce a downward pressure on prices. Two considerations, nevertheless, lead one to think that they could. First, as defenders of the petroleum industry have historically maintained, the prices of petroleum products are highly elastic with regard to supply.[20] Thus, relatively small amounts of new production brought on line could have a dramatic downward effect on prices. Second, if French petroleum firms did not have to weigh the opportunity costs of exploration—particularly in marginal areas—against possible returns from other, less risky, investment, they might pursue exploration more willingly. (This was exactly the original French policy in Algeria.) Thus it would not be unreasonable to expect that public enterprise, unconstrained by a profit motive, could have a significant effect on prices, especially if the "scarity" of petroleum has been exaggerated.[21] In any event, there is very little to lose. Under current conditions, corporations constrained to maximize profits have little incentive to find more than the most marginal new barrel of oil—and have every incentive to claim that that barrel is all there is left to find.

It might, of course, be argued that high domestic oil prices serve important purposes. They encourage conservation, reduce the demand for imported oil, and indirectly ease pressure on the balance of payments. However, this at best is a two-edged sword. Even if the

---

[20] This was meant to justify oil cartels. Cf. Paul H. Frankel, *Essentials of Petroleum* (London: Frank Cass, 1969), p. 86 and John Blair, *The Control of Oil* (New York: Vintage Books, 1976), p. 77. The drop in oil prices after 1981 seemed to confirm this.

[21] It should be noted that the post-1981 oil glut, essentially manufactured by Saudi Arabia's refusal to limit production during a world recession, does not by itself rule out future scarcity, but one does suspect that fears of a rapid decline of reserves are exaggerated.

economy eventually adjusts to the inflationary boost of high oil prices (which in the short term weakens the franc), by raising the macroeconomic cost structure, higher-than-world-market energy prices reduce French competitive capacity.[22] If this in turn encourages dependence on nuclear energy, the result may be a long-term high cost economy that will encourage pressure for even more protectionism. The point should be made, however, that high oil prices have consistently been defended by policy makers as maintaining the profitability of French oil companies and, by extension, France's security of supply. Once again the findings of this study reveal that if this indeed is the reason for high petroleum prices, the activities of the independent state companies do not support the official explanation.

Managerial Autonomy. It is, of course, concern for efficiency that has been the principal justification for allowing French public enterprises their large degree of managerial autonomy, the understanding being that profit centers encourage efficiency and avoid unintended subsidies.[23] The idea is, quite simply, that firms need a flexible management to respond to ever changing market conditions. Flexibility therefore requires a decentralization of authority. It is this decentralization of authority that I have termed "managerial autonomy."

It should be noted that the widespread acceptance of managerial autonomy and profit maximization for public firms is in many ways a justifiable reaction to past experience. Public enterprises have frequently wasted resources when inattention to costs was not only possible, but recurrent. The lack of attention to costs leads to many kinds of waste, including free spending of foreign exchange, featherbedding, and often monumental boondog-

[22] See Cohen, "Informed Bewilderment," pp. 38–39.
[23] Simon Nora, *Rapport sur les Entreprises Publiques* (Paris: Documentation Française, 1967), pp. 26ff.

gles. It was the free-spending habits of the SNCF (the French rail company) that led the authors of the Nora Report to recommend profit maximization. Moreover, managerial autonomy without the discipline of the bottom line leads to the worst of all possible worlds, as the catastrophic activities of Mexico's PEMEX or Indonesia's Pertamina testify.[24]

However, profit maximization and managerial autonomy as guarantors of efficiency only make sense in a competitive environment. Although some public firms *are* in competitive markets and have done well as quasi-independent profit maximizers, they are precisely the firms for which *public* enterprise was not needed in the first place (see Chapter 1). If public enterprise is a genuine corrective to market imperfections, by definition market incentives will not alone ensure the efficient allocation of resources. Conversely, it is not clear from the point of view of pure logic why public firm executives could not be rewarded for cost-minimizing rather than profit-maximizing behavior. The success of this approach seems clear in the example of TVA cited above. In imperfectly competitive markets, which increasingly characterize western economies, a cost-centered approach would seem an obvious choice.

In a real sense, the efficiency criterion that justifies managerial autonomy is a throwback to Adam Smith's "invisible hand": the assumption is that an economy composed of individual profit-maximizing firms will benefit from the most efficient use of available resources. Like many such abstractions, this one ignores the obvious: imperfect competition cannot be assumed away. Allowing managers to behave as if their environment resembled that envisioned by a textbook does not solve the distortions of concentrated markets. Concentration means individual firms have market power—the power to influence prices and production. In the end such influence has political

[24]I am grateful to an anonymous reader for Princeton University Press for pointing this out to me.

ramifications. In short, market power is *political* power. Political considerations cannot be divorced from an understanding of economic phenomena.[25] However, changing economic conditions are the death knell of managerial orthodoxies. It would appear that the era of Alfred P. Sloan is over.[26] There is at best a dynamic tension between the need to ensure the efficient allocation of resources at the microeconomic level (via managerial autonomy) and the need to ensure the public weal. This goes beyond the prescriptions of collective goods theorists who accent the compatibility of public goals and individual profit.[27] In the real world, the microeconomic concern with efficiency of public firms can lead to the creation of independent centers of power. As we have seen, far from optimality, the result is a collection of warring fiefs. One may say, only slightly facetiously, that French state capitalism has brought back feudalism.

Thus relieving French nationalized oil industry of the need to maximize profits, while allowing for some return on investment, would both remove incentives for corporate behavior that runs counter to public policy goals and eliminate the justification for the creation of irresponsible centers of power. Deemphasizing profit maximization erodes the justification for public firm autonomy.

This solution is all the more enticing because it focuses on a problem that is common to other administrations. As

[25] Note the reproving tone of John Kenneth Galbraith's "Power and the Useful Economist," *American Economic Review* 63 (March 1973). On this point see also François Morin, *La Structure Financière du Capitalisme Français* (Paris: Calmann-Lévy, 1974), p. 276; and François Perroux, *Pouvoir et Economie* (Paris: Bordas, 1973).

[26] Sloan, the innovative president of General Motors, pioneered the organization of firms as collections of profit centers.

[27] The most well-known of these is Mancur Olson, *The Logic of Collective Action* (Cambridge: Harvard University Press, 1965). This approach has become very popular for students of American politics. For a recent primer, see Norman Frolich and Joe A. Oppenheimer, *Modern Political Economy* (Englewood Cliffs: Prentice-Hall, 1978), pp. 33ff.

noted in Chapter 5, the rise of the "state-within-a-state" syndrome of public enterprise is recurrent in Western Europe. Others have also taken note of this proliferation of "ungovernable" centers of power:

> As "hiving off," or creating *débudgetisé* public organizations, has become a popular response to the problems of public management, we must also be cognizant that this response may, in fact, lessen the ability of those nominally in charge of government to manage what happens in the public sector, and may, therefore, ultimately make government less, rather than more manageable.[28]

It should be noted that *autonomy* and *control* are poles defining a spectrum of government-company relations. The mix should be adjusted for the characteristics of each sector in which a firm operates. Although the evidence for reducing managerial autonomy is clearest in the petroleum sector, the logic applies to any sector with substantial departures from the competitive model. To the extent that developed economies are marked by increasing degrees of concentration (see Chapter 1), one would expect social concerns to dictate an increasing degree of public control.

The issue of government control of state-owned enterprise is certainly complex. Yet although both academic economists and public officials constantly trumpet the disadvantages of interfering with a public firm's management, the dysfunctions of managerial autonomy are only rarely signaled.[29] Are they strangely obtuse? Rather, I think this assymetry can be understood by examining the political backdrop to the debate.

[28] B. Guy Peters, "Bureaucracy, Politics and Public Policy," *Comparative Politics* 11 (April 1979), p. 347.

[29] For an article refreshingly concerned with this issue, see William G. Shepherd, "Objectives, Types, and Accountability," in *Public Enterprise: Economic Analysis of Theory and Practice*, ed. William G. Shepherd (Lexington, Mass.: Lexington Books, 1976).

Où Est l'Etat? Qu'est-ce que l'Etat?

Posing a hypothetical alternative to present French public sector policy is by itself a rather sterile exercise. What makes the trip down the path not taken worthwhile is the extent to which the exercise illuminates the path that *was* taken. What constrains decision makers from pursuing some paths? Assuming that French policy choices were not simply accidental, the examination of alternatives should reveal a network of constraints on those who exercise public authority. This is another way of examining the autonomy of the state.

STATE, SOCIETY, AND CAPITALISM

Constraints upon the actions of public authorities have been the subject of a recent and highly abstract body of literature. Rooted in nineteenth-century sociology, the concern with the state's relation to civil society has been popularized anew by a diverse set of theorists, including marxists of both structuralist and instrumentalist bent, and conservative writers associated with the neomercantilist school of political economists.[30] It is this body of scholarship that has shaped this study.

A focus on constraints may somewhat bias the inquiry as it betrays a concern with structure,[31] but the very widespread recurrence of decentralized public sector organization suggests a focus on what these cases have in common, especially the fundamentally capitalist organization

[30] See Chapter 1 of the present study. Marx and Engels trace the distinction to the early capitalism of the eighteenth century (*bürgerliche Gesellschaft*): "Civil society as such develops with the bourgeoisie" (Karl Marx and Friedrich Engels, *The German Ideology* [New York: International Publishers, 1980], p. 57). Perry Anderson traces the dualism to Machiavelli in "The Antinomies of Antonio Gramsci," *New Left Review* 100 (November 1976–January 1977), p. 20. See also Chapter 1, notes 40, 41, and 42.

[31] David A. Gold, Clarence Y. H. Lo, and Erik Olin Wright, "Recent Developments in Marxist Theories of the Capitalist State," part 2, *Monthly Review* 27 (November 1975), p. 37.

of their economies. Thus the argument to follow returns to the themes of Chapter 1 to assess the value of particular explanations in accounting for the problems of French public enterprise. The argument sketches the limits of culture and elite theories to explain present French policies, and then explores various economic interest explanations. Finally, it traces the links between state and society revealed by the failure of the French state to control nationalized firms. One can only understand the failures of French policy by viewing the state as intimately linked to society, and it is this link, endemic to all capitalist countries, that limits the power of the state.

POLITICAL CULTURE

Citizens' attitudes toward authority are a frequent explanation of French difficulties.[32] Can culture in some way account for the lack of control of public enterprise? Two considerations suggest that it cannot. First, the characteristics usually associated with French political culture should encourage a predisposition *against* managerial autonomy. Both statism and a tradition of highly centralized authority would lead one to expect public officials to be at least uncomfortable with the decentralization of the public sector. Certainly, there has been a debate in France about the extent of decentralization: the liberal-*dirigiste* debate in the context of oil policy. But this has taken place among discussants who *share the same culture*. Of course, it may be argued that French political culture, which originally facilitated the acceptance of state intervention, also serves to

[32]Michel Crozier repeats the theme of his early work on bureaucracy to explain the European disarray of the 1970s in his chapter entitled "Western Europe," in *The Crisis of Democracy* by M. Crozier, S. Huntington, and J. Wantanuki (New York: New York University Press, 1975). Crozier argues that the state's very autonomy, necessary to mediate relations between individuals, alienates citizens who see the state as too detached from society, and thus are made ripe for persuasion by communists. Crozier is one of the few conservatives to view (inadvertently) the relationship of state to society as dialectical.

restrain decentralization and that public firms would have even greater leeway in the absence of cultural inhibitions. This is hard to resolve, but among the countries examined in Chapter 5, nowhere is public enterprise more decentralized than in France.

Conversely, public sector organization and behavior have been similar in countries of different political cultures. The antipodal cultures of Britain and Italy, to name only two of the cases discussed in Chapter 5, produced essentially the same problem: autonomous managers pursued profit at the expense of the public interest.

ELITE THEORY

A more serious set of arguments relies on elite explanations of public firm behavior. As noted before, the peculiar characteristics of the French administrative elite tend to complicate both the formulation and implementation of purely rational economic policies.[33] Once there is a fragmentation of interests within the elite, it is not unreasonable to expect a fragmentation of the state, which is composed of institutions populated by competing elites. Thus, the functional decentralization of the state, both in the organization of the administration and in the relationship of public firms to the administration, may be a means of accommodating conflicting elite interests.[34] In this line of reasoning, the problems that a ministry has in eliciting specific behavior from a public firm may be the result of the regulators' and company executives' loyalties to opposing Grands Corps. Conversely, the collaboration of public and private firms may be vastly facilitated by com-

[33] That is, "rational" from the point of view of neoclassical economics.

[34] This has in fact been suggested in the work of Nicos Poulantzas, although the elite are taken to represent the interests of various factions of capital. See George Ross, "Nicos Poulantzas, Eurocommunism, and the Debate on the Theory of the Capitalist State," *Socialist Review* 9 (March-April 1979). This is a review of Poulantzas's last book, *State, Power and Socialism* (New York: New Left Books, 1978).

mon corps affiliations and the informal contacts such affiliations imply.

The elite approach does, however, pose some problems. As we noted in Chapter 4, French Grands Corps behavior combines elements of both competition and cooperation. Since the episodes of competition tend to occur when prestigious career positions are at stake, it is difficult to explain debates in terms of elite conflict when the stakes do not involve—or do not appear to involve—carving up the career pie. To some extent, one can account for the appearance of new firms in terms of elite career needs, but Elf's and CFP's refusal to obey directives of an agency populated by their "own" corps members goes unexplained.

Nor does the comparative aspect of this study support an elite explanation for the similarities of public enterprise behavior across national frontiers. It is true that some countries, such as Italy and Spain, have similar administrative corps, but others, Britain and Austria for example, do not. Of course the latter may be beset by other forms of elite conflict, since divisive issues may vary from country to country. Thus explanations of conflict become ad hoc and each issue of division is treated sui generis. A series of independent explanations based on elite theory might be accurate for each conflict between national administration and its recalcitrant public enterprise, but this would be complicated, perhaps needlessly so. In social science, as in the physical sciences, one finds virtue in parsimony.[35]

[35]Note the emphasis on the principle of parsimony in Peter Alexis Gourevitch's elegant "International Trade, Domestic Coalitions and Liberty: Comparative Responses to the Crisis of 1873–1896," *Journal of Interdisciplinary History* 8 (Autumn 1977), pp. 281–313. The sectoral analysis that follows was suggested by the work of Gourevitch and James R. Kurth. This kind of analysis, implicitly, can also be found in James Pool and Suzanne Pool, *Who Financed Hitler?* (New York: Dial Press, 1979). Most of these works find their intellectual origins in Alexander Gerschenkron's *Bread and Democracy in Germany* (Berkeley: University of California

There is, however, no problem in identifying Britain, France, Austria, Italy, and the other countries of Western Europe as fundamentally capitalist. This is not only because the publicly owned sector in all of these countries is small compared to their respective private sectors but, more importantly, because the organization of incentives and the economically productive relationships in the public sectors of these countries are indistinguishable from the private sectors. As the incentives and relationships in the public sector mirror those in the private sector, the term that most aptly describes public enterprise in these countries is "state capitalism."[36] The nature of ownership in Western Europe has not affected firm behavior.

How does the basic organization of the economy explain both the support for French petroleum policy and the problems associated with public enterprises that French policy is meant to protect? I have outlined in the preceding pages the advantages of a non-profit-maximizing corporation in the petroleum sector. If one wishes to explain why the option has not been chosen, several answers are possible. The first would explain the lacuna by simply assuming those responsible for policy to be myopic or stupid. Although such a contention might be marvelous grist for a political mill, this kind of elite explanation would have trouble accounting for why an elite that owes its recruitment to academic merit would not at least consider a seemingly obvious solution.

This is a particularly interesting question in light of the arrival of the Mitterrand government in 1981. Nationalization formed the centerpiece of the Socialists' economic policies, but it was clear that if they conceived of nationalization any differently from their predecessors, the distinction either was kept a secret or was one of the subtlest

Press, 1943) and in the tradition of German historiography more generally.

[36] There is no general agreement on the meaning of this term. Cf. Stuart Holland, *The Socialist Challenge* (London: Quartet Books, 1975).

161

nuance. An official French press release emphasized that:

The Mitterrand administration believes that government involvement in the nationalized companies must be kept to a minimum, and provisions on management in the nationalization law clearly reflect this philosophy. The phrase "Renault-style management" has been used to describe their intention to leave the day-to-day affairs of the company to its executives, in much the same way that the auto manufacturer has been operated since its nationalization.[37]

Indeed, one of the pre-election slogans was *"Nationalisation,* but not *Etatisation,"* reaffirming the Socialists' commitment to managerial autonomy.

If we consider the Mitterrand government as an electoral elite within a fundamentally capitalist context, we are confronted with a situation where a policy (in this case, of managerial autonomy and profit maximization) remains constant although the elite changes. Once again this sug-

[37] "Documents from France," no. 82/35 (Press and Information Service of the French Embassy, March 1982, mimeograph), p. 10. The commitment was reaffirmed, although with an important nuance, by the Industry minister's letter to the presidents of the newly nationalized firms: "The usual management criteria for industries will apply in their entirety to your groups: your various activities should show a level of profitability *sufficient to ensure the expansion of the company and a normal return on capital"* ("Documents from France," no. 82/35, annex, p. 1; emphasis added). Theoretically, the terms "sufficient to ensure expansion" and "normal return on capital" could imply a fixed return similar to that of a public utility. However, the fact that the letter was signed by Pierre Dreyfus, a champion of managerial autonomy and profit maximization, suggests that "normal" behavior is to be profit maximization. The ambiguity of the wording is important, for it may in fact be a manifestation of compromise vocabulary worked out between different factions of the Socialist government.

Indeed the government was divided between "minimalists" such as Dreyfus and "maximalists" such as Technology minister Chevènement, who urged greater control over the nationalized sector (Cf. *Business Week,* 28 September 1981). This in turn suggests explanations that disaggregate the state.

gests that a focus on elites does not yield a satisfying independent variable. References to economic variables are more illuminating. However, economic influences may take many forms. One possible way of tracing them is to examine the needs of various sectors of the French economy.

ECONOMIC SECTORAL APPROACH

Such an explanation would take into consideration the coalitions of interests that stand to gain from present policy. If one examines the direct interests of specific sectors of the French economy, it is easy to see who is disadvantaged by France's high-priced oil and independent public firms. Energy intensive industries, especially those that depend upon export markets, are clearly losers. The steel industry, for instance, has been at a considerable disadvantage worldwide, but nowhere more so than in France.[38] So too the domestic auto industry, with the notable exception of Renault, whose sales of fuel-efficient small cars have prevented it from suffering the fate of Peugeot, Citroën and Chrysler.[39] Independent petrochemical firms, which must buy their raw materials from oil companies, also suffered.[40]

Of course labor, whose jobs are held hostage, has also done poorly in these sectors. Although labor is theoretically a substitute factor for energy, every indication is that labor, particularly where it is weakly organized (e.g., most sectors in France), has suffered more from oil-induced inflation and recession than it has gained from job substi-

[38] The French solution here was a partial nationalization (i.e., a bailout) by Giscard, which was completed under Mitterrand. Cf. *Wall Street Journal*, 21 September 1978.

[39] See the interview with Renault's president, Bernard Vernier-Palliez, in *Paris Match*, no. 1624, 11 July 1980.

[40] Formerly private Rhone-Poulenc has even accused U.S. petrochemical firms of unfair competition because of cheaper U.S. domestic oil prices (*Wall Street Journal*, 14 October 1980). Rhone-Poulenc was nationalized and its petrochemicals went to Elf (*Le Monde*, 13 May 1982).

tution.[41] Both labor and management in competitive sectors, where cost increases cannot easily be passed along, have also clearly lost.[42]

Certainly, those who have had the most to gain are the energy sector itself, including substitute energy such as nuclear and allied industries, and high technology industries such as armaments, which are capital intensive but not energy intensive.[43]

A sectoral analysis seems to indicate an overwhelming coalition in opposition to the present petroleum policy and to the organization of the public sector that abets high-priced petroleum. Presumably, democratically elected officials should reflect these interests.

Although bureaucratic resistance might explain how elected officials representing this "anti-oil" coalition could be stymied in their attempts to change the policy, the evidence does not support this. No politician in power has ever really articulated a policy that could be said to reflect the interests of the anti-oil coalition. Attempts by the Giscard-Barre government to impose *liberalisme* might have reduced prices in the short term by eliminating the costs of protectionism, but it is hard to see any long-term gains from such a policy "change." Moreover, this kind of analysis does not explain how the essentially dysfunctional structure of public enterprise remains or why a Socialist government, which one would assume to be committed to the interests of the anti-oil coalition, should in fact be divided on the issue. The prevailing Socialist view favors the incentives of managerial autonomy and profit maximization.[44]

[41] See the discussion in Sanford Rose, "The Far-Reaching Consequences of High-Priced Oil," *Fortune* 89, no. 3 (1974), p. 191.

[42] See note 1 above.

[43] France's effort to offset its oil bill with arms and nuclear exports bears this out. Cf. *Wall Street Journal*, 19 November 1980; and Stephen S. Cohen, "Informed Bewilderment."

[44] *Business Week*, 28 September 1981, p. 42.

That present French policy seems to show no evidence that a low-price coalition has developed may point up a weakness in this sectoral analysis. Partially this is due to its functionalism: determining the objective needs of a sector is considered sufficient as an explanation for the political outcomes.[45] However, the different sectors may not accurately perceive their own interests. Those who are hurt by French oil policy do not perceive that policy as the culprit and thus do not act to change it. This at first might appear unlikely, since the very substantial literature on interest groups suggests that such groups are very quick to recognize their own interests.[46] Nevertheless, it is my contention that in normal times[47] groups accept broad "rules of the game" within which they promote their interests, and that a "low-price" outcome could only be achieved by transgressing the "rules" of received economic wisdom. These tenets govern the management of the French and, indeed, all western economies.

ECONOMIC STRUCTURE AND ORTHODOXY

There is a link between the failure of public enterprise and the fact that the failure has gone unrecognized. (Parliamentary criticisms, from the Right or Left, have never challenged the *organization* of public enterprise.) To present a conflict between profit maximization and the possibility of achieving any macroeconomic optimum is to

[45] Peter Gourevitch partially avoids this difficulty by substituting "situation" for "objective interest." See his "Breaking with Orthodoxy: The Politics of Economic Policy Responses to the Depression of the 1930s," *International Organization* 38 (Winter 1984), p. 98.

[46] This work is perhaps the best achievement of students of American politics. For a subtle application of it to the study of foreign economic policy see Theodore Lowi, "American Business, Public Policy, Case-Studies and Political Theory," *World Politics* 16 (July 1964).

[47] In crisis situations groups often will be willing to promote systemic change. See David Abraham, *Collapse of the Weimar Republic* (Princeton: Princeton University Press, 1981), chap. 6 and *passim*. For the process by which this occurs see Peter Gourevitch, "Breaking with Orthodoxy."

challenge the prevailing orthodoxy. The point here is that adherence to the neoclassical economic principles which underlie the present organization of the public sector can be construed as an *ideological* commitment of the regime. Can this ideological commitment be related to economic interests?

Marxists, of course, assume that the dominant ideology reflects the interests of the dominant class.[48] Structural marxists, particularly the followers of Louis Althusser, rely on the (functionalist) assumption that ideology mystifies class rule and thereby bolsters the position of the ruling class.[49] They take *The German Ideology* as their point of departure to develop their notion of ideological domination.[50] Thus an elaborate scheme of "ideological institutions," comprising most institutions of socialization (e.g., schools and churches), is developed to explain why people in capitalist societies do not rebel against their alleged oppression.[51] Gramsci's notion of hegemony extends the function of ideology to include the role of enforcing cohesion within the ruling class by imbuing the fragments of the ruling class with the same world view, thus ensuring the rule of the hegemonic fraction: "Ideology provides the 'cement' in a social formation, 'preserving the ideological purity of the entire social bloc.' "[52]

Ideology links state to society as well as uniting the rul-

[48] Marx and Engels, *The German Ideology.*

[49] See Chapter 1, note 40.

[50] "The *practical* struggle of these particular [class] interests, which constantly *really* run counter to the communal and illusory communal interests, makes *practical* intervention and control necessary through an illusory 'general' interest in the form of the State" (Marx and Engels, *The German Ideology,* p. 54).

[51] This notion of ideology is primarily associated with the work of Louis Althusser. Althusser's tortured language is made somewhat more intelligible in Stuart Hall, "Culture, the Media and the 'Ideological Effect,' " in *Mass Communications and Society,* ed. James Curran, Michael Gurvitch, and Janet Woolacott, (Beverly Hills: Sage Publications, 1977).

[52] Gramsci, quoted in Hall, "Culture, the Media and the 'Ideological Effect,' " p. 333; cf. Anderson, "The Antinomies of Antonio Gramsci."

ing class. A common *Weltanschauung* was seen by Marx in *The Eighteenth Brumaire* as a way of uniting the political representatives of the bourgeoisie, who as employees of the state were not themselves bourgeois, with the interests of the ruling class. It is here that constraints on perception link the state to class interest:

> Just as little one must imagine that the democratic representatives are all shopkeepers or enthusiastic champions of shopkeepers. According to their education and their individual position they may be separated from them as widely as from heaven and earth. What makes them representatives of the petty bourgeoisie is the fact that in their minds they do not go beyond the limits which the latter do not go beyond in life, that they are driven theoretically to the same tasks and solutions to which material interest and social position practically drive the latter. This is in general the relationship of the political and literary representatives of a class to the class they represent.[53]

Although Marx's reference is to the Parliament of nineteenth-century France, the link of state to society is insightful and relevant. Moreover, Parliament may incorporate a host of political representatives of various factions,[54] but the bureaucracy is more homogeneous. The recruitment patterns, education, and socialization described in Chapter 4 ensure even less ideological diversity in the bureaucracy than in Parliament.

Ideology reinforces institutional linkages of state to society. Thus the ideology of neoclassical economics dominates the solutions of French officials. This is reinforced

[53]Marx, quoted in Fred Block, "The Ruling Class Does Not Rule; Notes on the Marxist Theory of the State," *Socialist Review*, no. 33 (1977), p. 11. On the issue of representation of class interest in periods of crisis see Abraham, *Collapse of the Weimar Republic*, chap. 6.

[54]It is this reproduction of society's factions that paralyzes the Second Republic and leads to Napoleon III's coup in Marx's *Eighteenth Brumaire*.

by networks of dependence. In the French state, the political representatives depend on the bureaucracy for expertise and the bureaucracy depends on the private sector both for information and for the careers of its personnel. Those who do not accept the doctrine are not "serious," and are treated accordingly.

A caveat, however: ideology may be the mechanism that both unifies diverse factions and ensures the predominance of the private sector, but it does not necessarily follow that economic beliefs will function in the long-term interests of those who hold them. The evidence presented here seems to indicate that although the ruling ideology is based on an idealization of the market, its effect in terms of practical policy is to obscure solutions to the problems of advanced capitalism.

Ideology does indeed mystify, but what many writers seem to ignore is that ideology mystifies the rulers as well as the ruled. The metaphor of the atomized market that allows one to shuttle easily between economic and political concepts (e.g., "consumer sovereignty" or "the marketplace of ideas") mystifies economic relationships as thoroughly as it masks the reality of power. Thus when French officials base their strategies on an economic theory that assumes competitive markets, the consequences may do anything but shore up their hold on political power.

As we noted earlier, the choices made by French officials to establish and promote the managerial autonomy of public firms and to encourage them to maximize profits have accentuated inflationary pressures and disadvantaged many sectors of the French capitalist class. It appears that ideological assumptions about the nature of the market guided their choices. In this case, if the "function" of ideology is social cohesion,[55] the effects are social disruption. Why, then, do the doctrines hold sway?

Clearly, part of the reason is that an elite steeped in

[55] Nicos Poulantzas, *Political Power and Social Classes* (London: New Left Books, 1973), p. 209.

neoclassical training could hardly be expected to call the profit incentive into question quickly, even if they were not intent upon completing their careers in the private sector. Long-held ideas are relinquished as a last resort. As long as realities are not too harsh (the French economy is not yet on the verge of collapse) and while competing orthodox explanations hold at least a modicum of reason, the ideologies of the status quo will hold.

Yet the election of the Socialists in 1981 would seem to be rather problematic. If an ideological commitment to neoclassical economics explains the failure of state officials to assert political control over public firms, how does one impute the same explanation to elites who are supposedly skeptical of the market?

The first response to this is that the key decision makers in the Socialist administration are those most convinced of the value of the market, and that these members of the new elite are social democrats, not socialists.[56] Such a judgment requires caution, however. Even if the less market-oriented members of the Mitterrand cabinet had not been eclipsed by the "moderates,"[57] the Socialists were still dependent on the bureaucratic elite steeped in the neoclassical education of the Grandes Ecoles.[58]

Yet the underlying reality of Socialist power was precisely the moderation of their views. They were able to get elected and assume power, it could be argued, precisely because they offered moderate reform rather than radical

[56] Finance minister Delors and Planning minister Rocard fit this category, while former marxist Chevènement who replaced Dreyfus at the Ministry of Industry was applauded by the business community for his shift to pragmatism (*Business Week*, 10 January 1983); Philippe Simonnot adds Budget minister Fabius, advisor Attali and Mitterrand himself to the list (*L'Expresse*, 3 December 1982).

[57] *Business Week*, 28 September 1981.

[58] Ezra Suleiman, lecture to the Foreign Service Institute, U.S. Department of State, Spring 1982. Note especially that Mitterrand's principal economic advisor, Jacques Attali, was a professor at Ecole Polytechnique.

169

change. This recalls Block's argument that left-wing reformist governments are ultimately constrained by the need to elicit the confidence of business. If not, they risk an investment strike, capital outflow, and balance of payments difficulties that ultimately require the remedy of a full-scale austerity program and the retraction of initial reforms.[59] This is a structural mechanism that tethers the state to the needs of capitalist accumulation despite the elites' preferences for reform and redistribution. Thus even Socialists, who might have preferred a major change in the organization of the oil industry, would risk the loss of business confidence if public corporations were not run like "serious businesses."[60]

However, the interviews with members of the Socialist party conducted for this study suggest the last concern to be academic. No one interviewed saw a need for changing the organization of public firms.

STRONG STATES, WEAK STATES, AND CAPTURED STATES

The focus of much of the discussion in this study has been to relate the existence of public enterprise to conceptions of strong and weak states, and autonomous and subordinate states. Certainly, one constraint on state authorities has been the way they perceive problems and conceive of solutions. Acceptance of a neoclassical world view blinds leaders to solutions that might reduce social and economic tension, just as surely as such views bind them to the existing order of society.

In a broad sense, the state is linked to society by its ideology. Certainly, if the ideology favors particular classes or groups, policy conceived through that prism should also

[59] Block, "The Ruling Class Does Not Rule," pp. 144ff.; Charles Lindblom's treatment of business as a special interest is remarkably similar in *Politics and Markets* (New York: Basic Books, 1979), chap. 12; Anderson emphasizes the ultimate coercive power of the bourgeoisie ("The Antinomies of Antonio Gramsci," pp. 75ff).

[60] *New York Times,* 22 November 1981.

CONCLUSION

favor the already privileged. Yet there is a difference between the long and short term. The findings of this study
seem to point to a long-term inability of neoclassically organized public firms to solve the problems of advanced
industrial society, at least the problem of reasonably priced
or secure sources of oil. The quandary of French capitalism over managerial autonomy and profit maximization is
clear. The problem of questioning profit incentives in the
petroleum industry precisely shows the ramifications of the
case: if it is an unfettered profit-maximizing orientation
which leads to the collaboration of public firms with private oligopolists, then the logic is easily extended to other
concentrated sectors. If such incentives lead to perversion
of the public purpose in oil, why not in other industries?
One can hardly expect the private sector to applaud a
nonprofit competitor in their midst. Ideology is in a sense
the secret weapon of the private sector in keeping the state
at bay, or at least in minimizing state incursions.

Thus, the most famous phrase of *The German Ideology,*
that "the ideas of the ruling class are in every epoch the
ruling ideas" is an accurate but inadequate description of
the link between the society and its elected managers. For
although it is the acceptance of certain ideas which ensures that economic policymakers will be taken "seri-
ously" both by the electorate and by the holders of economic power, these same ideas vitiate the long-term
effectiveness of the state's economic policy. It is a final irony
that the ideological sinews which bind the state to capitalist society also inhibit it from solving the economic
problems of advanced capitalism. Neither the private sector nor the state capitalist public sector seems to have an
incentive structure that promises an easy solution to the
problems of energy, reindustrialization, and inflation.

What is the state? Where is the state? The Schvartz
Commission was not wrong to ask the latter, but first we
must respond to the former. The early (instrumentalist)
marxist characterization of the state as an "executive com-

171

mittee of the bourgeoisie" does little to illuminate the complex phenomenon and collection of contradictions that is the state. *"L'état n'est pas un château-fort,"* Poulantzas would reiterate to his classes near the Château de Vincennes.[61] Not to consider public enterprises as part of the state would seem to deny the origin of their existence, an existence rooted in a mercantilist state's response to the economic problems of society.

FRAGMENTATION OF THE STATE

Mercantilism, however, assumes a unified state pursuing a unified interest. But neither society nor the state is in any way uniform. Some sectors of society are more economically successful than others, and therefore their bargaining positions vis-à-vis the state are better. The complexity of economies requires a complexity in the state and in its policies. The very need for sectoral policies fragments the state into sectoral bureaucracies (e.g., the Ministries of Industry, Agriculture, and Labor). To put this in the context of our study of the policy process, the system of elite recruitment and the rewards of serving a successful sector, which has much to offer in *pantouflage*, makes some sectoral bureaucracies particularly vulnerable to the demands of the already privileged. Thus even within the capitalist class rich sectors get richer, poor sectors get poorer. The resulting fragmentation of the state, then, not only reflects the fragmentation of society, but it also reinforces and exaggerates it. Successful sectors win policies that reinforce or extend their advantages. In times when successful sectors are weakened due to exogenous factors like recessions or oil gluts, other sectors may momentarily gain advantages that translate into new institutions. Thus public firms appear when the private sector is weak or divided, but the imperatives of capitalist organization limit the extent to which the state institutions can intervene.

[61] Nicos Poulantzas, lectures at the University of Paris at Vincennes, 1977–1978.

Said another way, market forces fragment capitalist interests (e.g., into buyers and sellers, oligopolists and competitive industries) and become reflected in the state through a division of labor in the policy process. This fragmentation is reinforced by competition among elites whose corps have colonized different sectors. The dominant ideology of "efficiency-promoting" profit centers justifies independent firms and thus reinforces the fragmentation of the state. Thus, even when some sectors pass into public hands, the doctrines of profit maximization and managerial autonomy serve to keep the state from posing any real threat to the private sector as a whole.

The marxist literature on the "relatively autonomous" capitalist state accents *autonomous* in order to explain the success of government intervention and capitalist survival.[62] The theoretical intentions of these writers seem to be governed largely by embarrassment at the continuing ability of capitalist economies to endure. Yet their implicit conclusion is that the autonomous state ensures capitalism's durability.

The conclusions of this study are quite the opposite. It is precisely because the state is not autonomous that the problems of capitalist economies become intractable. Potentially powerful state institutions become neutralized. Strong states become weak states precisely because they are captured states.

The French state is strong, but it is not autonomous. It has had little trouble imposing high prices on French consumers while demanding sacrifices from those least able to resist. It has done nothing to extract concessions from the oil industry. As we have seen, the pattern is repeated in other sectors. Thus the state's management of the economy ultimately reflects and reinforces the fragmentation of society. The only unifying bond, that of ideol-

[62] See especially Theda Skocpol, "Political Responses to Capitalist Crisis: Neo-Marxist Theories of the State and the Case of the New Deal," *Politics and Society* 10, no. 2 (1981).

ogy, idealizes the market and in the end only exaggerates the centrifugal forces of French society.

Are public enterprises part of the state? Certainly they represent a tool by which the public interest can be imposed upon a portion of the private sector. But the doctrine of managerial autonomy severs the tool from the state and offers it to the sector of society meant to be controlled. Public enterprise represents the potential for society to take control of its economic destiny, but that potential has remained undeveloped. The Schvartz Commission inquired, "Where is the state?" They had good reason to ask.

BIBLIOGRAPHY

Books, Articles, and Government Documents

Abraham, David. *The Collapse of the Weimar Republic*. Princeton: Princeton University Press, 1981.

Adelman, M. A. "The Multinational Corporation in World Petroleum." In *The International Corporation*, edited by Charles P. Kindleberger. Cambridge: M.I.T. Press, 1970.

————. *The World Petroleum Market*. Baltimore: Johns Hopkins University Press, 1972.

Allison, Graham. *The Essence of Decision*. Boston: Little, Brown, 1971.

Anderson, Perry. "The Antinomies of Antonio Gramsci." *New Left Review*, no. 100 (November 1976-January 1977).

————. *The Lineages of the Absolutist State*. London: Verso, 1975.

Archibugi, Franco, Jacques Delors, and Stuart Holland. "Planning for Development." In *Beyond Capitalist Planning*, edited by Stuart Holland. New York: St. Martin's, 1978.

Ball, George. "Cosmocorp: The Importance of Being Stateless." In *World Business: Promise and Problems*, edited by Courtney C. Brown. New York: Macmillan, 1970.

Berle, A. A., Jr. *Power without Property*. New York: Harcourt, Brace and World, 1959.

Berle, A. A., Jr., and G. C. Means. *The Modern Corporation and Private Property*. New York: Macmillan, 1932.

Blair, John. *The Control of Oil*. New York: Vintage Books, 1976.

————. *Economic Concentration: Structure, Behavior and Public Policy*. New York: Harcourt Brace Jovanovitch, 1972.

Block, Fred. "The Ruling Class Does Not Rule: Notes on the Marxist Theory of the State." *Socialist Review*, no. 33 (1977).

de Bodinat, Henri-René, and Michel Chambaud. "L'Influence de l'Etat sur le Secteur Pétrolier Français." *Revue Française de Gestion*, no. 10 (May-June 1977).

Bridges, Amy Beth. "Nicos Poulantzas and the Marxist Theory of the State." *Politics and Society* 4 (Winter 1974).

Carré, J.-J., P. Dubois, and E. Malinvaud. *French Economic Growth.* Translated by John P. Hatfield. Stanford: Stanford University Press, 1975.

Casanova, Jean-Claude. *Principes d'Analyse Economique.* Paris: Les Cours de Droit, 1968–1969.

Catta, E., and E. Lemasson. "Le Vote de la Loi de 1928." Note de Synthèse, Nouvelle Série, no. 2. Paris: Compagnie Française des Pétroles, Service de Documentation, 7 November 1977. Mimeograph.

Chenot, Bernard. "Les Paradoxes de l'Entreprise Publique." *Revue Française de Science Politique* 5 (October–December 1955).

Chevalier, Jean-Marie. *Le Nouvel Enjeu Pétrolier.* Paris: Calmann-Lévy, 1973.

Cohen, Stephen S. "Informed Bewilderment." In *France in the Troubled World Economy,* edited by Stephen S. Cohen and Peter A. Gourevitch. London: Butterworth, 1982.

————. *Modern Capitalist Planning: The French Model.* Berkeley and Los Angeles: University of California Press, 1977.

Comité Professionel du Pétrole. *Petrole 77.* Paris: Comité Professionel du Pétrole, 1978.

Commission d'Enquête Relative à l'Organisation du Monopole des Pétroles. *Journal Officiel* (Paris: Documentation Française, 3 February 1928).

Crozier, Michel. *The Bureaucratic Phenomenon.* Chicago: University of Chicago Press, 1964.

————. "Western Europe." In *Crisis of Democracy,* by Michel Crozier, Samuel P. Huntington, and Joji Wantanuki. New York: New York University Press, 1975.

Delors, Jacques. "The Decline of French Planning." In *Beyond Capitalist Planning,* edited by Stuart Holland. New York: St. Martin's, 1978.

Destler, I. M. *Presidents, Bureaucrats, and Foreign Policy: The Politics of Organizational Reform.* Princeton: Princeton University Press, 1974.

Ehrmann, Henry W. *Politics in France.* 3rd ed. Boston: Little, Brown, 1976.

Engler, Robert. *The Brotherhood of Oil.* Chicago: University of Chicago Press, 1977.

Faure, Edgar. *Le Pétrole dans la Paix et la Guerre.* Paris: Editions de la Nouvelle Revue Critique, 1939.

Feigenbaum, Harvey B. "EC Industrial Policy and Implications for the U.S." Bureau of International Commerce, U.S. Department of Commerce, Washington, D.C. 1972. Mimeograph.

———. "France's Oil Policy: The Limits of Mercantilism." In *France in the Troubled World Economy*, edited by Stephen S. Cohen and Peter A. Gourevitch. London: Butterworth, 1982.

———. "Public Enterprise in Comparative Perspective." *Comparative Politics* 15 (October 1982).

François-Marsal, Frédéric. *Le Dépérissement des Entreprises Publiques*. Paris: Calmann-Lévy, 1973.

Frankel, Paul. *Essentials of Petroleum*. London: Frank Cass, 1969.

———. *Mattei, Oil and Power Politics*. New York: Praeger, 1966.

Frolich, Norman, and Joe A. Oppenheimer. *Modern Political Economy*. Englewood Cliffs: Prentice-Hall, 1978.

FTC Report, *see* U.S. Federal Trade Commission.

Gabet, C., and G. Honoré, and F. Houssin. "Les Répercussions Mécaniques des Hausses des Prix Energétiques." *Economie et Statistique*, no. 56 (May 1974).

Galbriath, John Kenneth. *Economics and the Public Purpose*. New York: New American Library, 1975.

———. "Power and the Useful Economist." *American Economic Review* 63 (March 1973).

Garner, M. R. "The White Paper on Nationalised Industries: Some Criticism." *Public Administration* 5 (Spring 1979).

George, Alexander L. *Presidential Decisionmaking in Foreign Policy: The Effective Use of Information and Advice*. Boulder, Co.: Westview Press, 1980.

Gerschenkron, Alexander. *Economic Backwardness in Historical Perspective*. New York: Praeger, 1962.

Gilpin, Robert. "The Political Economy of the Multinational Corporation: Three Contrasting Perspectives." *American Political Science Review* 70 (March 1976).

———. *U.S. Power and the Multinational Corporation*. New York: Basic Books, 1975.

Giscard d'Estaing, Valéry. *French Democracy*. Translated by Vincent Cronin. New York: Doubleday, 1977.

Gold, David A., Clarence Y. H. Lo, and Erik Olin Wright. "Recent Developments in the Marxist Theories of the Capitalist State." Parts 1, 2. *Monthly Review* 27 (October, November 1975).

Gourevitch, Peter Alexis. "Breaking with Orthodoxy: The Politics of Economic Policy Responses to the Depression of the 1930s." *International Organization* 38 (Winter 1984).

————. "International Trade, Domestic Coalitions and Liberty: Comparative Responses to the Crisis of 1873–1896." *Journal of Interdisciplinary History* 8 (Autumn 1977).

Granfield, Michael. "Concentrated Industries and Economic Performance." In *Large Corporations in a Changing Society*, edited by J. Fred Weston. New York: New York University Press, 1975.

Green, Mark J., B. C. Moore, and B. Wasserstein. *The Closed Enterprise System*. New York: Grossman, 1972.

Groupe de Travail du Comité Interministériel des Entreprises Publiques, *see* Nora, Simon.

Hall, Stuart. "Culture, the Media and the 'Ideological Effect.' " In *Mass Communications and Society*, edited by James Curran, Michael Gurvitch, and Janet Woolacot. Beverly Hills: Sage Publications, 1977.

Hartshorn, J. E. *Politics and World Oil Economics*. New York: Praeger, 1967.

Heclo, Hugh. "Issue Networks and the Executive Establishment." In *The New American Political System*, edited by Anthony King. Washington, D.C.: American Enterprise Institute, 1978.

Heilbroner, Robert. "The Post-Keynesians." *The New York Review of Books*, 21 February 1980.

Herberg, Mikkal. "Planning, Politics and Capitalism: National Economic Planning in Britain and France." *Political Studies* 29 (December 1981).

Hoffmann, Stanley. "Paradoxes of the French Political Culture." In *In Search of France*, by Stanley Hoffmann, Charles P. Kindleberger, Lawrence Wylie, Jesse R. Pitts, Jean-Baptiste Duroselle, and François Goguel. New York: Harper & Row, 1962.

Holland, Stuart. "Adoption and Adaptation of the IRI Formula: Britain, France, Canada, Australia, Sweden, West Germany." In *The State as Entrepreneur*, edited by Stuart Holland. New York: International Arts and Sciences Press, 1972.

————. "The Finance Formula." In *The State as Entrepreneur*, edited by Stuart Holland. New York: International Arts and Sciences Press, 1972.

————. *The Socialist Challenge*. London: Quartet Books, 1975.

————. "State Entrepreneurship and State Intervention." In *The State as Entrepreneur*, edited by Stuart Holland. New York: International Arts and Sciences Press, 1972.

Hubert, René. "Le Problème du Pétrole devant le Parlement." *Revue Politique et Parlementaire* 143, 427 (10 June 1930).

Huntington, Samuel P. *Political Order in Changing Societies*. New Haven: Yale University Press, 1968.

Huré, J. "La Politique Française du Pétrole, I." *Revue des Deux Mondes*, 16 April 1966.

Johnson, Carol. "Relations with Government and Parliament." In *The State as Entrepreneur*, edited by Stuart Holland. New York: International Arts and Sciences Press, 1972.

Judet, Pierre. "La Détérioration des Relations entre la France et l'Algérie." *Le Monde Diplomatique*, February 1976.

Katzenstein, Peter J. "Conclusion." In *Between Power and Plenty*, edited by Peter J. Katzenstein. Madison: University of Wisconsin Press, 1978.

————. "International Relations and Domestic Structures: Foreign Economic Policies of Advanced Industrial States." *International Organization* 30 (Winter 1976).

————. "Introduction." In *Between Power and Plenty*, edited by Peter J. Katzenstein. Madison: University of Wisconsin Press, 1978.

Kaysen, Carl. "Business and Government: Do Good Fences Make Good Neighbors?" Paper presented at a symposium on business-government relations of the American Bankers Association, Washington, D.C., 1 April 1966.

Kemp, Tom. *Industrialization in Nineteenth-Century Europe*. London: Longman, 1969.

Kindleberger, Charles P. "The Postwar Resurgence of the French Economy." In *In Search of France*, by Stanley Hoffmann, Charles P. Kindleberger, Lawrence Wylie, Jesse R. Pitts, Jean-Baptiste Duroselle, and François Goguel. New York: Harper & Row, 1962.

Kornhauser, William. *The Politics of Mass Society*. New York: Free Press, 1959.

Krasner, Stephen D. *Defending the National Interest*. Princeton: Princeton University Press, 1978.

————. "A Statist Interpretation of American Oil Policy toward the Middle East." *Political Science Quarterly* 94 (Spring 1979).

————. "Trade in Raw Materials: The Benefits of Capitalist Alliances." In *Testing Theories of Imperialism*, edited by Steven R. Rosen and James R. Kurth. Lexington, Mass.: Lexington Books, 1974.

Kuisel, Richard F. *Ernest Mercier, French Technocrat.* Berkeley and Los Angeles: University of California Press, 1967.

Landes, David. "French Business and the Businessman: A Social and Cultural Analysis." In *Modern France: Problems of the Third and Fourth Republics*, edited by Earl Meade. New York: Russell and Russell, 1964.

Lazarus, Simon. "Halfway Up from Liberalism: Regulation and Corporate Power." In *Corporate Power in America*, edited by Ralph Nader and Mark Green. New York: Grossman, 1973.

Lehmbruch, Gerhard. "European Neo-Corporatism: An Export Article?" Woodrow Wilson Center, Washington, D.C., 26 April 1982.

Lévy, D.M.G. "Control of Public Enterprise in France." In *Government Enterprise*, edited by W. Friedmann and J. F. Garner and translated by J. F. Garner. London: Stevens and Sons, 1970.

Lindberg, Leon N. "Comparing Energy Policies: Political Constraints and the Energy Syndrome." In *The Energy Syndrome*, edited by Leon N. Lindberg. Lexington, Mass.: Lexington Books, 1978.

Lindblom, Charles E. *Politics and Markets.* New York: Basic Books, 1979.

Lord, Guy. *The French Budgetary Process.* Berkeley and Los Angeles: University of California Press, 1973.

Lowi, Theodore. "American Business, Public Policy, Case Studies and Political Theory." *World Politics* 16 (July 1964).

Lucas, N.J.D. "The Role of Institutional Relationships in French Energy Policy." *International Relations* 5 (November 1977).

McConnell, Grant. *Private Power and American Democracy.* New York: Vintage Books, 1966.

Magdoff, Harry. *The Age of Imperialism* New York: Monthly Review Press, 1969.

Marois, Bernard. "Le Comportement Multinational des Entreprises Françaises Nationalisées." *Revue Française de Gestion* (March-April 1977).

Marx, Karl. *The Eighteenth Brumaire of Louis Bonaparte.* New York: International Publishers, 1963.

Marx, Karl, and Friedrich Engels. *The German Ideology*. New York: International Publishers, 1980.

Mendershausen, Horst. *Coping with the Oil Crisis*. Baltimore: Johns Hopkins University Press, 1976.

Michalet, Charles-Albert. "France." In *Big Business and the State: Changing Relations in Western Europe*, edited by Raymond Vernon. Cambridge: Harvard University Press, 1974.

Miliband, Ralph. *The State and Capitalist Society*. London: New Left Books, 1969.

"Le Monde Pétrolier en 1928." *Pétrole Informations*, no. 1464 (23 February–1 March 1978).

de Montaigne, René. "Présence Pétrolière de la France au Proche Orient." *Revue Française de l'Energie*, no. 215 (October-November 1969).

Moore, Barrington, Jr. *Social Origins of Dictatorship and Democracy*. Boston: Beacon Press, 1966.

Morin, François. *La Structure Financière du Capitalisme Français*. Paris: Calmann-Lévy, 1974.

Murat, Daniel. *L'Intervention de l'Etat dans le Secteur Pétrolier Français*. Paris: Technip, 1969.

Nora, Simon. Groupe de Travail du Comité Interministériel des Entreprises. *Rapport sur les Entreprises Publiques*. Paris: Documentation Française, April 1967. Cited as Nora Report.

Nove, Alex. *Efficiency Criteria for Nationalised Industries*. Toronto: University of Toronto Press, 1973.

―――. "Recent Developments in Eastern European Economics." In *Post Industrial Society*, edited by Bo Gustafsson. London: Croom Helm, 1979.

Nussenbaum, Maurice. "Comment Controller la Gestion des Entreprises Publiques?" *Le Monde*, 19 March 1977.

O'Connor, James. *Fiscal Crisis of the State*. New York: St. Martin's, 1973.

Olson, Mancur. *The Logic of Collective Action*. Cambridge: Harvard University Press, 1965.

Organization of Petroleum Exporting Countries. *Selected Documents of the International Petroleum Industry 1968*. Vienna: OPEC, 1969.

Perrous, François. *Pouvoir et Economie*. Paris: Bordas, 1973.

Peters, B. Guy. "Bureaucracy, Politics and Public Policy." *Comparative Politics* 11 (April 1979).

Phillips, Almarin. "Introduction." In *Promoting Competition in Regulated Markets*, edited by Almarin Phillips. Washington, D.C.: Brookings Institution, 1975.

Pinkney, David. "The French Experiment in Nationalization, 1944–1958." In *Modern France: Problems of the Third and Fourth Republics*, edited by Earl Meade. New York: Russell and Russell, 1964.

Pool, James, and Suzanne Pool. *Who Financed Hitler?* New York: Dial Press, 1979.

Posner, M. V., and S. J. Woolf. *Italian Public Enterprise.* Cambridge: Harvard University Press, 1967.

Posner, Richard. "Theories of Economic Regulation." *Bell Journal of Economics and Management Science* 5, no. 2 (1974).

Postan, M. M. *An Economic History of Western Europe from 1945 to 1964.* London: Methuen, 1967.

Poulantzas, Nicos. *Political Power and Social Classes.* London: New Left Books, 1973.

———. *State, Power and Socialism.* New York: New Left Books, 1978.

Prodi, Romano. "Italy." In *Big Business and the State*, edited by Raymond Vernon. Cambridge: Harvard University Press, 1974.

Pryke, Richard. *The Nationalised Industries.* Oxford: Martin Robertson, 1981.

Rheinstein, Max. "Introduction." In *Max Weber on Law in Economy and Society*, edited by Max Rheinstein and translated by Edward Shils and Max Rheinstein. New York: Simon and Schuster, 1967.

Robinson, Joan. *Economic Heresies: Some Old Fashioned Questions in Economic Theory.* New York: Basic Books, 1971.

Robock, Stefan H. "An Unfinished Task: A Socio-Economic Evaluation of the TVA Experiment." In *The Economic Impact of TVA*, edited by John R. Moore. Knoxville: University of Tennessee Press, 1967.

Rondot, Jean. *La Compagnie Française des Pétroles.* Paris: Plon, 1962.

Rose, Sanford. "The Far-Reaching Consequences of High-Priced Oil." *Fortune* 89, no. 3 (1974).

Ross, George. "Nicos Poulantzas, Eurocommunism, and the Debate on the Theory of the Capitalist State," *Socialist Review* 9 (March–April 1979).

Rustow, Dankwart. "Europe in the Age of Petroleum." In *Indus-*

trial Policies in Western Europe, edited by Steven J. Warnecke and Ezra Suleiman. New York: Praeger, 1975.

Saad, Farid W. "France and Oil: A Contemporary Economic Study." Ph.D. diss., Massachusetts Institute of Technology, 1969.

Safer, Arnold. *International Oil Policy.* Lexington, Mass.: Lexington Books, 1979.

Sampson, Anthony. *The Seven Sisters.* London: Coronet Books, 1975.

Saumon, Dominique, and Louis Puiseux. "Actors and Decisions in French Energy Policy." In *The Energy Syndrome,* edited by Leon N. Lindberg. Lexington, Mass.: Lexington Books, 1978.

Schumpeter, Joseph. *Capitalism, Socialism and Democracy.* New York: Harper Colophon Books, 1975.

Schvartz, Julien. *Rapport sur les Sociétés Pétrolières Opérant en France,* Assembleée Nationale, Annexe au procès-verbal de la séance du 6 novembre 1974, no. 1280 Paris: Documentation Française, 1974. Cited as Schvartz Report.

Shell, Kurt. *The Transformation of Austrian Socialism.* New York: State University of New York Press, 1962.

Shepherd, William G. "British and United States Experience." In *Public Enterprise: Economic Analysis of Theory and Practice,* edited by William G. Shepherd. Lexington, Mass.: Lexington Books, 1976.

―――. "Objectives, Types, and Accountability." In *Public Enterprise: Economic Analysis of Theory and Practice,* edited by William G. Shepherd. Lexington, Mass.: Lexington Books, 1976.

Shonfield, Andrew. *Modern Capitalism.* New York: Oxford University Press, 1969.

Simonnot, Philippe. *Le Complot Pétrolier.* Paris: Editions Alain Moreau, 1976.

―――. *Les Nucléocrates.* Grenoble: Presses Universitaires de Grenoble, 1977.

―――. *Le Pouvoir Monétaire.* Paris: Seghers, 1975.

Skocpol, Theda. "Political Responses to Capitalist Crisis: Neo-Marxist Theories of the State and the Case of the New Deal." *Politics and Society* 10, no. 2 (1981).

Slick, W. T. "A View from a Large Oil Company." In *Witness for Oil,* edited by M. E. Canes and P. M. Markun. Washington, D.C.: American Petroleum Institute, 1976.

BIBLIOGRAPHY

Sloman, Martyn. *Socializing Public Ownership*. London: Macmillan, 1978.

Smith, Adam. *An Inquiry into the Nature and Causes of the Wealth of Nations*. Oxford: Clarendon Press, 1976.

Steinbruner, John D. *The Cybernetic Theory of Decisions*. Princeton: Princeton University Press, 1974.

Stobaugh, Robert B. "The Oil Companies in the Crisis." *Daedalus* 104 (Fall 1975).

Stoffaës, Christian, and Jacques Victorri. *Nationalisations*. Paris: Flammarion, 1977.

Stucker, James P. "The Distribution Implications for a Tax on Gasoline." *Policy Analysis* 3 (Spring 1977).

Suleiman, Ezra N. *Elites in French Society*. Princeton: Princeton University Press, 1978.

————. "Industrial Policy Formulation in France." In *Industrial Policies in Western Europe*, edited by Steven S. Warnecke and Ezra N. Suleiman. New York: Praeger, 1975.

————. "The Myth of Technical Expertise: Selection, Organization, and Leadership." *Comparative Politics* 10 (October 1977).

————. *Politics, Power, and Bureaucracy*. Princeton: Princeton University Press, 1974.

Tait, Alan A., and David R. Morgan. "Energy and the Role of Gasoline Taxation." *Finance and Development* 17 (June 1980).

Tanzer, Michael. *The Political Economy of Oil and the Underdeveloped Countries*. Boston: Beacon Press, 1969.

Thoenig, Jean-Claude. *L'Ere des Technocrates: Le Cas des Ponts et Chaussées*. Paris: Editions d'Organisation, 1973.

de Tocqueville, Alexis. *The Old Regime and the French Revolution*. Translated by Stuart Gilbert. New York: Doubleday, 1955.

Turner, Louis. *Oil Companies in the International System*. London: Allen and Unwin, 1978.

Union des Chambres Syndicales de l'Industrie Pétrolière. "L'Industrie Française du Pétrole Répond." Paris: UCSIP, December 1974.

U.S. Federal Trade Commission. *The International Petroleum Cartel*. Washington: Government Printing Office, 1952.

Walters, Kenneth D., and R. Joseph Monsen. "State-Owned Business Abroad: New Competitive Threat." *Harvard Business Review* 52 (March–April 1979).

Weber, Max. *The Protestant Ethic and the Spirit of Capitalism.* New York: Charles Scribner's Sons, 1958.

Wilkins, Myra. *The Maturing of Multinational Enterprise.* Cambridge: Harvard University Press, 1974.

———. "The Oil Companies in Perspective." In *The Oil Crisis,* edited by Raymond Vernon. New York: W. W. Norton, 1976.

Wolf, Ronald H. "Identical Pricing and TVA: Toward More Effective Competition." In *The Economic Impact of TVA,* edited by John R. Moore. Knoxville: University of Tennessee Press, 1967.

Zeitlin, Maurice. "Corporate Ownership and Control: The Large Corporation and the Capitalist Class." *American Journal of Sociology* 79 (March 1974).

Zysman, John. *Governments, Markets, and Growth: Financial Systems and the Politics of Industrial Change.* Ithaca: Cornell University Press, 1983.

———. *Political Strategies for Industrial Order: State, Market and Industry in France.* Berkely and Los Angeles: University of Califronia Press, 1977.

Company Reports and Statistical Sources

Comité Professionel du Pétrole. *Eléments Statistiques.* Paris.

Editions Olivier Lesourd. *Guide du Pétrole.* Paris.

Entreprise de Recherches et d'Activités Pétrolières. *Rapport de Gestion.* Paris.

Compagnie Française de Pétroles. *Rapport de Gestion.* Paris.

Société Nationale Elf-Aquitaine. *Rapport de Gestion.*

———. *Reunion des Analystes Financiers et Représentants de la Presse Economique. Compte Rendu.* Paris: SNEA, 9 June 1977. Mimeograph.

Newspapers and Trade Journals

Business Week. New York.

Documents from France. Press and Information Service of the French Embassy. New York.

Les Echos. Paris.

The Economist. London.

L'Expresse. Paris.

Le Figaro. Paris.

The Financial Times. London.

185

BIBLIOGRAPHY

J'Informe. Paris.
Le Matin de Paris. Paris.
Le Monde. Paris.
The New Statesman. London.
The New York Times. New York.
Paris-Match. Paris.
Pétrole Informations. Paris.
Revue Pétrolifère. Paris.

The Times. London.
The Wall Street Journal. New York.
The Washington Post. Washington, D.C.
World Business Weekly. London.

INDEX

Achnacarry Agreement of 1928, 65, 66-67
Adelman, M. A., 35n, 42
Algeria, 69, 70, 77, 78-79. *See also* oil, Algerian crude
Anglo-Saxon Trust, 38
auditing, *see* state auditors
authority, citizens' attitudes toward, 158. *See also* public authorities
authority relations, 5

balance of payments, *see* foreign exchange problems
banks, nationalized, 132-35
Barre, R., 83, 164
Barre Plan, 45
Berle, A. A., 13
Blair, J., 67
Block, F., 170
Bonnefous Commission, 93
British Petroleum (BP), 122, 123-24
bureaucrats, *see* civil servants

capital: encouraging flow of, 17; outflow of, 151; state economic intervention and, 11, 12; state ownership and costs of, 20. *See also* financing; investment
capital goods, French industrialization and, 10-11
capitalism, durability of, 173; state, 161
capitalist economies, nonautonomous state and problems of, 173

Cartel des Dix, 37, 40, 56
cartelization, disincentives to, 151-53
cartels, 65; Achnacarry Agreement and, 66-67; competition and, 36-37; delegated monopoly and, 40; disputes among partners in, 94; French tolerance and promotion of, 11; government-managed, 19, 40, 42; justification for, 35n; market failure and, 35-37; petroleum industry and, 34; prices and, 36, 42, 44
CFP, *see* Compagnie Française des Pétroles
Chalandon, A., 74, 83, 84, 106, 148
Charbonnel, J., 78
civil servants, 103-105. *See also* elites; Grands Corps
commissaires, see commissioners
commissioners, government policy and, 95
Commission of Inquiry into Nationalized Industry, 93
Compagnie Française des Pétroles (CFP), 55, 122; Achnacarry Agreement and, 65-66; Algerian contracts of, 79; Corps des Mines and, 107; lack of extensive state auditing of, 93; Mexican contract and, 85; origins of, 56-58; promotions in, 107; proposed merger with Elf, 80-82, 107; reluctance to search for Saharan oil, 60; role of, 61-62, 64-68
competition: cartels and, 36-37,

maximization of, 121, 131, 132, 149, 155; Socialists and, 164
profit margins: of French refineries, 51; transfer of pricing authority and, 45
property, control and power and, 13
Proporz, 133
protectionism: autonomy of the state and, 53; domestic impact of, 51-53; strength of the state and, 53
Pryke, R., 136
public authorities, constraints on actions of, 157-58
public enterprise: autonomy of the state and, 22-26; capitalist economies and, 137; choice of managers for, 27-28, 104-105; definition of, 3; failings of, 136; failure of, 165; as instrument of national economic policy, 140; lack of control over, 26; market concentration and, 26; political control of, 138; regulation of, 129-30; as state capitalism, 161; as substitute for planning, 21, 128; where private sector is weak, 20. *See also* public firms
Public Enterprise Accountability Commission, 93
public firms, 12-22; auditing of, 93, 95-96; behavior of, 22-26, 154; competition and, 26; *contrats de programmes* and, 28n; control of, 77, 95, 156; investments in other companies and, 29-30; politicization of, 27; profit maximization and, 25; public goals and, 71-85, 114; purpose of, 21; sectoral interests and, 25; as sources of accurate information, 149-50; as

state intervention, 21; state represented on boards of, 95; "success" of, 149; as yardsticks to measure private firms' performance, 147-49. *See also* public enterprise; state holding companies; state-owned oil companies
public-private sector conflict, 20, 85
public-private sector cooperation, 8, 68; elite career patterns and, 25, 104-105
public sector reorganization option, 147-57

reformist governments, constraints on left-wing, 170
reserves: Law of 1928 and three-month, 39, 43; security of supply and, 51-53. *See also* security of supply of petroleum
risk, state support to subsidize, 83
Robinson, J., 14, 15
Rocard, M., 149
Rotterdam spot market, 43n
Royal Dutch/Shell, 38

Sampson, A., 35-36
Schumpeter, J., 15
Schvartz Commission, 93, 174
Schvartz Report, 71-72, 117
security of supply of petroleum, 82; explorations by CFP and Elf and, 63; French petroleum policies and, 146-47; French public oil companies and, 123; high oil prices and, 153; managerial autonomy and, 83; meaninglessness of, 78; reserves and, 51-53. *See also* reserves

Library of Congress Cataloging in Publication Data

Feigenbaum, Harvey B., 1949–
The politics of public enterprise.

Revision of thesis (Ph. D.)—University of California, Los Angeles, 1981.
Bibliography: p.
Includes index.
1. Petroleum industry and trade—Government policy—France. I. Title.
HD9572.6.F45 1985   338.2'7282'0944   84-42883

ISBN 0-691-07677-4 (alk. paper)
ISBN 0-691-02229-1 (pbk.)